NURTURING

INNER

LOVE

A Journey of Self-Awareness

Val Kizza Ssegirinya

DECLARATION OF INTENT

I promise to honor my authentic self by nurturing inner love and being mindful of my thoughts, feelings, and actions. I commit to living fully present and open-hearted, embracing each moment with courage and compassion every time I engage with this book. Through this, I will deepen my self-awareness, cultivate inner peace, and build resilience to grow beyond limiting beliefs and activate my full potential.

I dedicate myself to this lifelong practice of building resilience, setting healthy boundaries, and embracing vulnerability as a source of strength. With honesty, kindness, and intention, I will live in harmony with my deepest values and highest potential, serving both myself and humanity.

This journey is mine, and I choose to walk it with patience, courage, and grace, knowing I am worthy of love, acceptance, and all of life's possibilities.

Sign:

_____

Date:

_____

TABLE OF CONTENT

CHAPTER 1 1
UNDERSTANDING INNER LOVE 1
   1.1 The Significance of Inner Love 2
   Real-Life Anecdotes and Personal Stories 4
   1.2 difference between inner love and narcissism 13
   1.3 Overcoming Anxiety with Inner Love 24
CHAPTER 2 32
BARRIERS TO INNER LOVE 32
   2.1 The Bitter Truth Personal story 57
   2.2 Thought Journal Exercise 58
CHAPTER 3 78
EMBRACING VULNERABILITY IN SELF-AWARENESS 78
   3.2 Practical Exercises 96
CHAPTER 4 115
PRACTICAL STEPS TO CULTIVATE INNER LOVE 115
CHAPTER 5 156
MINDFULNESS AND INNER PEACE 156
   Benefits of Mindful breathing 164
CHAPTER 6 184
HEALING PAST WOUNDS 184
CHAPTER 7 203

BUILDING POSITIVE RELATIONSHIPS 203
    7.1 Identifying and Nurturing Supportive Relationships 208
    Recognizing Supportive Relationships 208
    Relationship Audit activity 210
CHAPTER 8 221
SUSTAINING INNER LOVE 221
    8.1 The Self-Care Schedule 226
    8.3 A Lifelong Commitment 250
    8.4 The Beauty of Inner Love 259
REFERENCES 266

DISCLAIMER

Embarking on the journey of nurturing inner love is a deeply personal and transformative experience. This book provides valuable insights, strategies, and exercises to help you connect with yourself and cultivate empathy, in line with the Golden Rule: "Do unto others as you would have them do unto you" (Matthew 7:12). However, it is intended for informational and entertainment purposes only and should not replace professional mental health care.

The content in this book is based on personal experiences and general self-help practices. It is not tailored to individual mental health needs. Everyone's journey is unique, and what works for one person may not work for another. If any part of this book feels challenging, it may be a sign to seek support from a qualified therapist or mental health professional.

If you are facing severe emotional or psychological difficulties, please seek professional help immediately. The author and publisher are not responsible for any harm resulting from the use of this book. Combining its insights with professional care can help create a balanced approach to well-being. Always prioritize your mental health and seek support when needed.

ACKNOWLEDGMENTS

Creating this book has been a deeply satisfying experiences of my life, and it would not have been possible without the support, direction, and inspiration of so many wonderful individuals.

First and foremost, I extend my heartfelt gratitude to my family. Your resolute support and encouragement have been my rock. To my parents, thank you for instilling in me the values of kindness and self-worth, which have shaped the person I am today. To my siblings, your love and belief in me have been a source of strength, keeping me grounded through even the most challenging times.

To my friends, thank you for being my sounding board, offering honest feedback, and providing endless encouragement. Your companionship, laughter, and wisdom have been invaluable throughout this journey. A special thanks to those who shared their personal stories and insights, enriching this book with their experiences and making it even more relatable.

I am deeply grateful to my mentors and teachers, who have guided me on the path of self-awareness, mindfulness, and personal growth. Your wisdom and insights have been instrumental in shaping my understanding of inner love and emotional resilience. A special acknowledgment to Mubiru Jackson—your introduction to the world of fitness was more than just about physical discipline.

If not for your persistent encouragement and insistence that I push forward, even through muscle aches and fatigue, I wouldn't have cultivated the resilience that has carried me through uncertainty, including the journey of writing this book.

To my wonderful community of followers, your engagement and enthusiasm have fueled my passion. Your stories of personal transformation and reflections on my content have been a continuous source of inspiration. Thank you for allowing me to be part of your journey.

A heartfelt thank you to my editor, whose keen eye, thoughtful suggestions, and dedication have significantly elevated the quality of this book. Your hard work and commitment are deeply appreciated. To the entire team behind the scenes—the designers, proofreaders, and everyone who contributed to bringing this book to fruition—thank you for your professionalism and dedication.

Finally, to you, the reader—thank you for picking up this book. Your journey toward inner love and self-awareness is unique, and I am honored to be part of it. I hope this book serves as a meaningful companion, offering guidance, inspiration, and a reminder that you are deserving of love, understanding, and growth.

PREFACE

After embodying love through a profound journey of self-awareness and envisioning a future where humanity coexists harmoniously with AI agents, I experienced a life-altering revelation: the world is in desperate need of love. This realization illuminated a deeper truth—when we immerse ourselves in love by practicing creativity, personal accountability, mutual respect, understanding, empathy, and aligning with our deepest desires, we unlock the ability to navigate life's complexities, including those introduced by artificial intelligence, with ease and grace.

This book is born out of that revelation. It is not a collection of fragmented personal stories or a recounting of past relationships and experiences. Instead, it is a universal roadmap—a guide to inspire humanity to embrace self-awareness, embody love, and live harmoniously in an ever-evolving world. My hope is that this book ignite within you a transformation as powerful as the one I experienced.

I remember sharing the beta version of this book with a friend. As he flipped through its pages, he paused, looked at me with a smile, and asked, "What inspired you to write this book?" I took a deep breath, reflecting on the depth of my journey, and replied, "It's a long story, but in essence, people need to understand that creation—and the life we live—begins within our own conscious awareness. When we shift our perspective from victimhood, irresponsibility, and expectation to understanding, integrity, and creativity, we realize that our circumstances are merely reflections of our internal state. Through this mastery, we gain the ability to shape our lives and live harmoniously in a unified world." He raised his eyebrows and he thoughtfully said, "That sounds like not an easy task." I smiled and replied, "You're right—it's not easy. But change starts with oneself. It's like a feeling I can't feel for you. I can only imagine it, but experiencing it is entirely up to you. This book isn't about providing answers but about awakening what is already within you."

"Wow, that is profound," he responded, nodding. "If what you've told me is exactly what's in this book, it will inspire many people and touch countless lives." His words reignited my belief in this project, shifting my inner dialogue from self-doubt—"Am I wasting my time?"—to conviction: "The world is ready and waiting for my creativity."

Think of this book as your trusted companion—a friendly guide to accompany you on a transformative journey into the depths of inner love. Together, we will explore the ups and downs of life and discover what it means to truly love and accept ourselves—flaws, quirks, and all. This is not just another book. It is an invitation—a call to embark on a deeply personal journey that blends storytelling, introspection, and growth. If you are ready to step beyond conventional, evidence-based self-help and into a world where personal stories and lived experiences offer profound wisdom, then you are in the right place. Here, the journey is as important as the destination.

This book isn't about striving for perfection or cultivating narcissism. Instead, it's about finding that sweet spot where you can genuinely appreciate and embrace your authentic self, sharing it harmoniously with the world. It is crafted for those open to finding inspiration in unexpected places. Through a mix of life-inspired stories, reflections, and exercises, it encourages you to look inward, question long-held beliefs, and nurture a deeper sense of inner love and understanding.

To be clear, this book is not solely based on scientific studies to validate its insights. Instead, it speaks to the part of you that yearns for deeper meaning and connection. If you're someone who often seeks comfort in concrete facts and figures, you may find this journey to be a different kind of challenge—and that's a valuable opportunity.

You're invited to set aside, just for a moment, the need for rational proof and open your heart to the idea that emotional truths hold their own kind of wisdom. Think of this book as a mirror reflecting parts of yourself you may have overlooked or dismissed. It invites you to keep a journal as you read, capturing thoughts, feelings, and reflections that arise—especially those that challenge your rational thinking. You may discover that these moments of challenge are where your most profound growth begins.

If you approach these pages with curiosity rather than judgment, you may find they hold a unique kind of value. Even skepticism can serve as a doorway to exploring new perspectives and unlocking parts of yourself long hidden. Here, every doubt and every question is an opportunity to deepen your understanding of who you are and who you could become.

Each chapter is designed as a steppingstone on the path to self-awareness and inner love, offering:

1. Practical tips to help you cultivate inner love.
2. Reflective exercises to deepen your understanding of yourself.
3. Heartwarming stories that will make you smile, nod in agreement, and maybe even chuckle at the absurdities of life.

This book is more than just words on a page—it's a catalyst for personal transformation. I encourage you to read actively, write in the margins, pause and reflect, and most importantly, keep a journal. Use it as a tool to navigate the thoughts and emotions that surface as you read. Challenge yourself to go beyond the surface level and engage with what truly resonates—or what resists.

Whether you come to this book as a skeptic or a seeker, know that every step you take in exploring your inner world is a step toward nurturing the most important relationship of all—the one you have with yourself. Your inner world is essentially your conscious awareness here the conscious mind creates thoughts. These thoughts are absorbed by the subconscious mind which expresses them through your action and attitude. Embrace the unknown, welcome the discomfort of growth, and let this journey be a path toward a more expansive and loving view of yourself and the world around you.

CHAPTER 1

UNDERSTANDING INNER LOVE

Definition of Inner Love

Inner love, often referred to as self-love, is the unwavering embrace of your true self, especially when it feels like everything is falling apart. It's the gentle whisper of "You are enough," the calming deep breath, and the warm reassurance that grounds you when life feels heavy. Inner love isn't about forcing a smile or superficial positivity; it's a deep, intentional practice of self-awareness.

Now, you might be wondering, "What exactly is self-awareness?" Self-awareness is the conscious understanding of your own thoughts, emotions, behaviors, strengths, weaknesses, values, and beliefs. It's about being mindful of how you respond to different situations, understanding why you feel the way you do, and recognizing how your actions impact both yourself and others—Emotional Intelligence. Inner love is the steady inner voice that says, "You've got this," even in life's little disasters, like spilling coffee on your favorite outfit.

Inner love is about showing up for yourself in all your messy, beautiful, imperfect glory. It's about looking in the mirror and seeing someone worthy of kindness, compassion, and respect—not because of what you've achieved, but simply because of who you are in this moment. This kind of love empowers you to navigate life's ups and downs with grace, confidence, and authenticity.

1.1 The Significance of Inner Love

Inner love is the cornerstone of your mental, emotional, and physical well-being. It's the deep-rooted anchor that keeps you steady through life's inevitable storms, giving you a solid sense of self-worth and stability. By nurturing inner love, you create the fertile ground upon which a richer, happier, and more fulfilling life can grow.

Imagine building a house on a shaky foundation—it may look sturdy at first, but the moment a storm rolls in, it begins to crumble. In the same way, inner love is the solid foundation upon which a truly satisfying life is built, holding everything else in place. Without it, you may find yourself constantly grasping for validation from others, only to be left feeling empty and unfulfilled. Inner love means granting yourself the respect, kindness, and compassion that you naturally deserve, especially on the days when life feels heavy.

It's about leaning into your vulnerabilities, finding strength within them, and making choices that honor your authentic self. Once you establish this strong foundation of inner love, you'll be amazed at how everything else in your life begins to align and flourish.

Research by Kristin Neff, a pioneering psychologist in the field of self-compassion, emphasizes that self-love, characterized by kindness towards oneself in times of suffering, significantly enhances mental well-being. Neff's studies indicate that individuals who practice self-compassion experience lower levels of anxiety, depression, and stress. Once you have nurtured your inner love, you build a better emotional resilience and mental stability that helps you to effectively navigate life's challenges.

The field of positive psychology, spearheaded by researchers like Martin Seligman, emphasizes the importance of self-acceptance and inner love as crucial components of a fulfilling life. Seligman's PERMA model—comprising Positive Emotion, Engagement, Relationships, Meaning, and Accomplishment—highlights how cultivating a sense of self-worth and inner love can lead to enhanced well-being and flourishing. A study in *Psychological Science* stated that individuals who score high on measures of inner love and self-acceptance report greater satisfaction and fulfillment.

Inner love also correlates with your physical health outcomes. Research has shown that individuals who practice self-love are more likely to engage in health-promoting behaviors, such as regular exercise and healthy eating. This reinforces the idea that a strong foundation of self-love influences various aspects of life, including physical health. This is crucial if you aim to live a healthy and fulfilling life.

Real-Life Anecdotes and Personal Stories

Discovering Self-Worth

There was a time when I believed that the key to filling the void within me was wrapped in the luxurious fabrics of Versace and Prada. I thought that if I dressed like the fashion icons who radiated confidence and sophistication, I could capture some of that magic for myself. So, I adorned myself in high-end designer suits, expecting the admiring glances and compliments from friends and strangers alike to fill the emptiness I felt deep inside and yield to happiness.

For a while, they did. The praise and attention I received from those around me were like fleeting patches over a wound, but beneath the surface, I felt like an imposter, cloaked in expensive garments that could never fully hide my insecurities. The more I sought external validation, the hollower the echoes of those compliments became. The suits were exquisite, but they weren't enough to sustain the sense of self-worth I was desperately chasing.

After discovering that true contentment comes from within and needs consistent nurturing through mindful practices, the more fulfilled I became. These weren't instant fixes but gradual, patient work. I learned to sit with myself, to acknowledge my thoughts, reframe them for good, and extend kindness to the parts of me I had always tried to hide. Slowly, I began to unearth a sense of self-worth that had been buried beneath layers of designer fabric and self-doubt.

This shift was transformative. It was as if a switch had been flipped; I no longer needed external validation to feel whole. The once-coveted designer suits, now free from the weight of my expectations, became something else entirely—a celebration of who I was, not a cover for who I wasn't. When I slipped into a Versace or Prada suit, it wasn't about hiding behind a label anymore; it was about expressing the inner confidence I had finally cultivated.

The suits were no longer my armor—they were simply the adornments of a person who had discovered that true self-worth comes from within.

In this journey of self-awareness, I learned that:

1. True contentment stems from within.

2. Inner love is not about external validation but about embracing our unique qualities and flaws.
3. When we radiate inner love, we become unstoppable, confident, resilient, and unapologetically authentic.

Overcoming a Bad Day

Have you ever had one of those days when it feels like the universe is testing you—piling on challenge after challenge just to see if you'll break? I know that feeling all too well. I've been right there, in the eye of the storm, where everything that could go wrong did.

It all began innocently enough, wrapped in a love story that felt straight out of a fairy tale: rooms filled with laughter, stolen glances that seemed to stop time, phone conversations that lasted for hours, and kisses that felt like magic. But like all fairy tales, mine had its dark twist. I treasured that love so deeply and prefer to keep most of its story private. Instead, let me share how life's mysteries often come wrapped in unexpected situations, each event a piece of the grand masterpiece of our journey toward self-awareness.

One day, while I was at work embracing the power of productivity, my phone rang

"Hey, how's your day?" she asked.

"Great," I replied.

"Can you come over? I have something I need to tell you."

"Sure, I'll be there after work."

"Okay, see you then."

Without hesitation and grimacing like a monkey drawing from past experiences, I drove to her place. Parked my car, and I called, "Hey, I'm here."

"Let me come," she replied.

I waited…and waited. Did I say I waited? Yes, I did. Eventually, since I was friends with the security guard by then, he recognized me and buzzed me into the building. I made my way up to her apartment, only to find she had just gotten up to let me in.

"How did you get in?" she asked.

"The security guard buzzed me in."

"How are you?" I asked her.

"I'm good and still working on my coursework I need to finish and submit."

"Okay, go ahead," I emphasized.

"Let me make myself a cup of tea," I added.

I went to prepare tea, trying to stay cool. When I returned, she had finished and sat near me. She took a sip of my tea and said, "You didn't put sugar. You don't want it?"

"No, I don't want any," I replied.

She kept quiet for a moment, the tension thick in the air. Then she said the words that shattered my world: "I think this relationship is going nowhere, so I need more time and space to work on myself."

In that moment, my world cracked open. I remember the sensation vividly—the cold, hard truth settling in, as if someone had yanked the ground from beneath me. I vanished from the scene, needing time to process and reframe that one devastating line. But no matter how much I tried to rationalize it, a swarm of unwelcome thoughts rushed in: "Did I do something wrong?" "Was I not enough?" "Is this just some kind of game?" "Is this the point where I just cease to exist?"

I could have let those thoughts consume me. I could have let that moment define the rest of my life. But instead, I made a choice. I decided to step into the pain and face it head-on—like a warrior charging into battle without armor, armed only with the truth of who I was and the unyielding will to rise again. Did I let it break me? Absolutely not. Through desperation I dove headfirst into the world of self-improvement, devouring self-help books like they were the last lifeline to a better version of myself. Along the way it solidified to a mission—no, a crusade—to become the ultimate version of me, echoing the devastating line, "work on myself"—stronger, wiser, more resilient, both mentally and physically. "Was it all that easy," you may ask. Of course not, it too almost four years and to be sincere I didn't know that it was leading me to realization of wholeness.

I remember reading one book that led me to another, like a trail of breadcrumbs guiding me toward self-discovery. One particular book that marked a turning point for me was The Rational Male by Rollo Tomassi. He emphasized not just stopping with his material but continuing to read and expand one's understanding. This sparked a new perspective for me: self-knowledge as a never-ending quest to renew and reshape one's outlook on life. Another book that had a profound influence was The Unplugged Alpha by Richard Cooper. It inspired me to work on my physique, particularly focusing on building a well-defined upper body. With this newfound awareness, I stepped into the gym with a clear goal: to concentrate on my upper body strength.

Picture this: me, lifting weights, earbuds blasting motivational audiobooks, and occasionally jamming to the latest pop hits. I was a multitasking marvel, determined to rise from the ashes of heartbreak. Each rep, each mile, each drop of sweat was a step toward reclaiming my energy and spirit. Then, during one particularly intense workout, as "Eye of the Tiger" blared in my ears, the truth hit me like a lightning bolt. I felt a surge of love flowing freely within my heart, as if I were reliving my time with my ex-partner. Despite all my efforts to transform myself into an unstoppable force, I had been neglecting the most crucial relationship of all—the one with myself. It was like an internal standing ovation, the floodlights illuminating a stage I didn't know existed, where I finally stood alone in the spotlight.

Oscar Wilde, in his infinite wisdom, once said, *"To love oneself is the beginning of a lifelong romance."* There I was, sweaty and breathless on the gym floor, making a vow to embark on the most important journey of my life—a journey of inner love. Let me tell you, the romance with oneself? It's the kind of epic love story that deserves its own Netflix series—filled with twists, turns, and the ultimate triumph of discovering wholeness within. They say, "What doesn't kill you makes you stronger"—and isn't that the truth? The breakup could have shattered me. I once believed that losing love meant losing life, but discovering that same feeling of love within myself, after nurturing and caring for who I am, proved far more enriching and empowering. So, think back to that one intense emotional event you overcame. It might be the very chapter where your strength and freedom began to bloom. Sometimes, the most profound transformations come from the moments we thought would break us.

From that moment on, I decided to treat myself as the main character in a feel-good sitcom. I learned to laugh at my mistakes, dance in my pajamas at 3 AM (no audience needed), and remind myself that heartbreak can be one of life's funniest teachers—if you view it from the right angle. This doesn't mean pushing people out of your life; rather, it's a realization that emerges naturally through consistent effort, self-work, understanding, and greater self-awareness. So, when the universe throws everything, it has at you, pause and remember this: You have the power to rewrite the script. Choose to see the plot twist not as an end, but as the beginning of a new chapter—one where you become the hero of your own story.

The Power of Self-Acceptance

Mark spent years hiding his struggles, wrapping himself in a facade that seemed unbreakable. Fear of judgment kept him trapped in a life that felt safe on the outside but was exhausting and isolating within. Each day was a battle to maintain the image of someone who had it all together, while anxiety gnawed at him from the shadows.

One day, the weight of it all became unbearable. In a moment of desperation, Mark made a choice he'd been avoiding for years—he confided in a close friend. Heart pounding, he braced himself for the rejection he felt certain would follow. But instead, something extraordinary happened. His friend didn't turn away or judge; he listened with compassion and offered the support Mark had been longing for in silence.

That moment was a revelation. In opening up, Mark uncovered a strength he hadn't known existed—a strength that allowed him to connect with others in ways he'd never experienced before. The walls he had built to protect himself began to crumble, revealing a new truth: vulnerability wasn't a weakness, but a bridge to deeper, more authentic relationships.

By embracing his vulnerability, Mark didn't just find solace—he found connection. Despite all his efforts to transform into a powerhouse of achievement, he realized he had been neglecting the most crucial relationship of all—the one with himself.

> *"You yourself, as much as anybody in the entire universe, deserve your love and affection." – Buddha*

But Mark's story isn't just his own. It's a mirror for all of us—a reminder to pause, reflect, and consider where his journey resonates with our own.

> *"Know then thyself, presume not God to scan; The proper study of mankind is Man." – Alexander Pope*

Mark's story challenges you to break free from the fear that keeps you isolated and to embrace the power of vulnerability. It's in those moments of raw honesty that you truly connect with others and discover the strength to grow into your best self. Don't wait for the weight of your struggles to break you down. Open up, reach out, and let vulnerability be the key to unlocking the life you deserve.

1.2 difference between inner love and narcissism

Inner love and narcissism are frequently mistaken for one another, yet they are fundamentally distinct. Inner love fosters a healthy, balanced relationship with oneself, while narcissism is characterized by an excessive self-focus that often disregards the well-being of others.

Inner love is rooted in self-acceptance and compassion, while narcissism is rooted in lack of empathy and a pervasive need for admiration. Studies have shown that individuals with inner love experience healthier interpersonal dynamics and emotional resilience, while those with narcissistic traits tend to struggle with maintaining fulfilling relationships and face higher levels of interpersonal conflict and dissatisfaction.

Example of Inner Love

Lily spent years putting others before herself, believing that her worth was tied to how much she could give. She was always there for everyone, yet she felt drained and unfulfilled, as if she was living life on autopilot. Deep down, she struggled with a nagging emptiness, a voice that whispered, "Is this all there is?" She often questioned whether her constant giving was truly appreciated or if she was simply being taken for granted.

One day, after yet another sleepless night of worrying about everyone else's needs, Lily found herself standing in front of her bathroom mirror. The early morning light cast a soft glow, but it did little to hide the dark circles under her eyes and the fatigue etched on her face. She gazed into her own eyes and barely recognized the woman staring back. The vibrant spark that once defined her seemed to have faded. Her reflection showed not just physical exhaustion but a deeper weariness of the soul. A wave of realization washed over her as she thought, "I've lost myself trying to be everything for everyone else." It was in that moment she understood she was missing something essential—she was missing herself.

Determined to turn things around, Lily began to practice inner love in small, intentional ways. But the journey was not easy; she grappled with guilt every time she considered her own needs. Setting boundaries felt foreign and uncomfortable. The first time she said "no" to a request, her heart pounded, and anxiety washed over her. She worried, "Am I being selfish? Will they think less of me?" Yet, she knew that continuing to neglect herself would only deepen her unhappiness.

She started by acknowledging her worth, not as an endless giver but as a person deserving of her own kindness and care. Each day was a battle against her ingrained habits. She journaled her feelings, confronting the fear that had held her captive. Slowly, she learned to prioritize her well-being without the shadow of guilt looming over her.

Lily also reconnected with the things that brought her true joy. She remembered how much she loved painting as a child—the way the brush felt in her hand, the freedom of bringing colors to life on a blank canvas. However, picking up the brush again stirred up insecurities. "What if I've lost my touch? What if I'm not good enough?" Despite these doubts, she set aside time each week to pursue this passion, even when life got busy. Those initial strokes were shaky, but as she immersed herself, the colors began to flow, mirroring the awakening within her. The more she painted, the more she felt her spirit coming back to life.

Through these acts of inner love, Lily began to see herself not just as a caregiver, but as a vibrant, deserving individual. The internal critic grew quieter as she embraced self-compassion. She realized that taking time for herself wasn't selfish—it was necessary. By filling her own cup first, she found she had more to give to others, not from a place of depletion, but from a place of abundance and joy.

Lily's journey is a reminder that inner love isn't about grand gestures—it's about facing and overcoming the internal struggles that hold us back. It's about making small, consistent choices that honor who you are, even when it's difficult. It's about setting boundaries, pursuing your passions, and treating yourself with the kindness you so freely give to others.

Take a lesson from Lily. Acknowledge your fears and doubts, but don't let them dictate your actions. Start by finding what makes your heart sing, whether it's painting, reading, dancing, or simply taking a quiet moment at the beach with yourself. Set time aside for these joys, protect them fiercely, and watch as your life begins to transform. Remember, inner love isn't a destination; it's a practice—a commitment to showing up for yourself every day, in ways big and small. Embrace it, and you'll discover a wellspring of fulfillment and peace that radiates from within to every experience of your life.

Example of Narcissism

A Narcissist's Tension
John had always believed he was extraordinary. In every room, he imagined himself as the shining star—the one others should admire, envy, and even worship. He didn't just thrive on attention; he demanded it, inhaling every compliment like oxygen. Deep down, though, the admiration never felt like enough. No matter how much praise he received, there was always a gnawing emptiness he couldn't quite place. He brushed it off, convincing himself it was

because others simply couldn't appreciate his brilliance as fully as they should.

At social gatherings, John took command of the space as if it were his personal stage. Conversations became mere vehicles for him to assert his superiority, his accomplishments towering over the small, trivial stories of others. He'd laugh to himself as someone tried to share an achievement, cutting them off mid-sentence with a subtle, almost imperceptible sneer. Perhaps he thought, "Why waste time listening when my own story is far more fascinating?"

His eyes would glaze over as friends spoke of their lives—mundane details, really, compared to his. He'd wait, barely concealing his impatience, ready to jump back into the spotlight the second there was a lull in the conversation.

"That reminds me of when I became the youngest executive at my firm," he interjected as Mark mentioned his recent promotion. "Oh, that's...great, John," Mark replied, his enthusiasm dampened. Around them, others exchanged glances, their smiles strained.

John believed people hung on his every word, captivated by his brilliance. After all, he was the only one worth listening to.

But what John didn't see—what he refused to see—was the slow retreat of those around him. Faces once lit with interest began to dim, friends' smiles faltering as his self-absorption became too much to bear. One by one, they grew weary of the unrelenting barrage of his stories, all centered on him, all devoid of any real connection. His need to be adored was like a black hole, sucking the energy out of every interaction and leaving behind an emotional vacuum.

As you read this, you might find yourself imagining friends, acquaintances, or people who exhibit these narcissistic traits. Pause for a moment. Before you pass judgement, take a moment to reflect inwardly. Could these be traits you are unconsciously projecting outward? Remember, every person you encounter serves as a mirror, reflecting the dialogue you hold within yourself.

Still, John felt no need to change. In fact, he believed their distance confirmed his greatness. *Surely, they must feel inferior around me,* he mused. *How could they possibly relate to someone as extraordinary as I am?* Their inability to engage with him on his level was their failure, not his. He couldn't be bothered to waste his time with those who didn't fully recognize his value.

Yet, behind the confident façade, there were cracks. On the rare occasions when he was alone, his mind would drift to the awkward silences that had started to linger after his monologues—the glances exchanged between friends when they thought he wasn't looking, the excuses when he suggested meeting up.

"Sorry, I'm swamped with work," Sarah texted back.

"Maybe another time," Paul replied, without suggesting an alternative.

For a fleeting second, a sharp pang of doubt stabbed through him. Had he pushed too far? Had he said too much?

No. Impossible. The problem wasn't him; it was them. They were jealous and intimidated by his brilliance. That's what he told himself, anyway. It had to be true.

But deep inside, where he couldn't bear to look, John was terrified. He needed the constant adoration because, without it, the mask of superiority would crumble, revealing the fragile self-worth he worked so hard to conceal. The endless boasting wasn't just pride—it was a shield. A shield against the fear that if he stopped talking, if he let the conversation focus on someone else for too long, the world might see the truth: that behind the endless stories of triumph, John felt small.

Over time, John's circle of friends shrank. He couldn't understand why people pulled away from him, why relationships once full of laughter and ease now felt strained and brittle. He had always thought of himself as the one everyone wanted to be around, yet increasingly, he found himself alone, wondering where the adoration had gone.

In moments of loneliness, he'd scroll through social media, desperately searching for evidence of his greatness—old posts, past achievements—anything to fill the growing void. But it wasn't enough. It was never enough.

John's story is a portrait of narcissism at its most insidious. On the surface, his behavior appeared to be one of arrogance, self-assurance, and unshakable confidence. But beneath that bravado lay an aching need for validation—a hollow sense of self-worth built on the crumbling foundation of external approval. His relentless quest for admiration had pushed away the very people who could have offered him what he truly craved: authentic connection, not just for his accomplishments but for who he really was.

For John, the cost of his narcissism was isolation, leaving him trapped in a prison of his own making. His story is a reminder that true connection is not found in being superior to others but in the vulnerability of mutual respect and understanding. And until John learns to look beyond the mirror of his own ego, the emptiness will remain—an endless hunger for admiration that can never be fully satisfied.

Comparison Chart

Aspect	Self- Love	Narcissism
Definition	Healthy, balanced relationship with oneself	Excessive self-focus and need for admiration
Behavior	Kindness, empathy, and respect for oneself and others	Lack of empathy, arrogance, and sense of superiority
Motivation	Genuine self-care and personal growth	Seeking validation and admiration from others
Impact on other	Positive, nurturing relationships	Toxic, draining relationships
Example	Practicing mindfulness, setting boundaries, pursuing passions	Boasting, manipulating, and dismissing others' feelings

Role of Inner Love in Mental and Emotional Well-Being

Inner love has a reflective impact on our mental and emotional health. Imagine having an internal source of support that is always available, understanding, and on your side. This is the benefit of inner love, developing resilience and emotional balance.

When you cultivate inner love, you create a solid emotional foundation. This foundation is like a fortress that shields you from life's challenges - stress, anxiety, and depression. With inner love, you become more resilient and able to bounce back from failures and setbacks with grace and strength.

I once struggled with anxiety, depression, and self-doubt—especially after a breakup—feeling as though I was trapped on an emotional rollercoaster. But everything changed when I discovered the power of inner love. By turning inward and nurturing myself, I found strength and healing through:

1. Daily gratitude
2. Mindfulness and stillness
3. Self-forgiveness

As you continue this journey of self-awareness, you will be introduced to practices like gratitude journaling in chapter 4, mindfulness in chapter 5 and self-forgiveness in chapter 6

Why It Matters

Inner love is not just a nice-to-have; it's essential for a balanced and fulfilling life. It acts as your emotional backbone, supporting you in times of joy and sorrow, success and failure. By nurturing inner love, you create a life that is not only more resilient but also more vibrant and joyful.

1.3 Overcoming Anxiety with Inner Love

Emily grew up being called "Miss Skinny" by those around her—not just classmates, but even her own siblings joined in the teasing. She tried everything to put on weight: changing her diet, avoiding people who made hurtful comments, but no matter what she did, nothing worked. She felt trapped in her own skin, as if she wasn't enough. Her body wouldn't change, and over time, that discomfort sank deeper. It wasn't just about her appearance anymore; the more she tried to force her body to be something it wasn't, the more she started to lose herself. Eventually, the weight she carried wasn't on the outside—it was within her mind. Anxiety clung to her like a shadow, heavy and suffocating, always there.

Every decision Emily made was filtered through a need for approval, for validation. Her inner voice, once innocent, had turned cruel. She constantly compared herself to others, chasing an elusive version of perfection she thought would make her lovable. But that quest was exhausting, leaving her never at peace with who she was.

One day, she realized something had to change. She couldn't live in fear and self-criticism any longer. "I was tired of hating myself," she admitted softly. "Tired of constantly feeling like I wasn't enough." That exhaustion became her turning point. It wasn't dramatic—it was a quiet, steady decision to let go of the fight against herself.

Emily began small. She started with daily affirmations, even though they felt strange at first. "I am enough," she whispered to herself each morning, her voice shaky with disbelief. At first, it felt like a lie. But she kept saying it, hoping that one day she'd believe it. Little by little, the words she spoke began to shift her mindset. What started as a flicker of hope grew into a steady flame. She set boundaries, learned to say "no," and slowly stopped basing her worth on the approval of others. She recognized that her value wasn't tied to her body, her weight, or anyone's opinions of her. Her worth was intrinsically stem from her inner strength.

As weeks turned into months, Emily felt the anxiety that had gripped her for so long begin to loosen. The tightness in her chest eased, the restless nights faded. For the first time in years, she felt light—free. She wasn't chasing approval anymore; she had found something far more powerful within herself: love.

Emily's journey didn't happen overnight. It was slow, often painful, but it was real. Through her struggles, she discovered that inner love isn't about fixing yourself; it's about embracing who you are as a whole. It's about speaking kindly to yourself when the world doesn't. And most importantly, it's about realizing that you are enough, exactly as you are.

Her story is a reminder of how easily we get caught in cycles of self-doubt, measuring ourselves by standards that were never ours to begin with. We all carry invisible scars—the words, the expectations—that can turn into anxiety if we don't confront them. But like Emily, you don't have to carry that weight forever.

If you've ever felt the weight of anxiety, the pressure to be more, or the fear that you'll never be enough, pause for a moment. Start small. Whisper words of love to yourself, even if they feel awkward at first. Establish boundaries that protect your peace. Remember, you don't need to be perfect to be worthy of love—you already are. In Chapter 4, you will explore the transformative power of affirmations and learn how to incorporate them into your daily life.

1.Building Resilience through Inner love

Paul sat alone in his dimly lit apartment, the distant hum of the city a backdrop to his swirling thoughts. His career felt like a relentless series of failures—missed promotions, rejected proposals, opportunities slipping through his fingers. Each setback chipped away at his confidence, casting a long shadow over his sense of self-worth. With every unrealized goal, he sank deeper into feelings of inadequacy, convinced that he was defined by his failures.

The weight of disappointment pressed heavily upon him, making it hard to breathe. Sleepless nights were haunted by a nagging voice that whispered of his shortcomings. He withdrew from friends and family, isolating himself in a cocoon of self-doubt. The passions that once ignited his spirit had dimmed, replaced by a lingering sense of hopelessness.

One rainy evening, as Paul gazed out the window watching droplets race down the glass, a profound emptiness enveloped him. He realized he was tired—tired of feeling like a perpetual failure, tired of letting his past define him. In that moment of quiet desperation, a question surfaced: "What if I'm more than my failures?"

This simple thought was the spark he needed. It wasn't a dramatic epiphany but a quiet, resolute decision to see himself differently. Paul chose to embrace inner love, understanding that change had to start from within. He began acknowledging his strengths, even if they felt buried beneath layers of doubt. He recalled his unwavering determination—the times he'd persevered when others had given up. He remembered his creativity, how he'd turned near-failed projects into surprising successes with innovative solutions. He recognized his ability to connect with people, building relationships that had weathered many storms.

Most importantly, he saw his resilience—the inner strength that kept him moving forward, no matter how many times he had been knocked down. As a popular quote by Les Brown goes, "When life knocks you down, try landing on your back, because if you can look up, you can get up." It was Paul's resilience that enabled him to rise again.

Paul started journaling, writing down daily affirmations and moments of gratitude. At first, it felt unnatural, but slowly, the words began to resonate. He sought out new experiences that reignited his passions—taking up painting, joining a local hiking group, volunteering at a community center. These activities reconnected him with others and reminded him of the joy in simply living.

Reflecting on his achievements, he took pride in the successful projects he had led, the mentorship he had provided to colleagues, the positive changes his ideas had brought to his workplace. He began to see that his setbacks didn't erase these accomplishments; they coexisted, painting a fuller picture of his journey.

As weeks passed, a transformation unfolded. By focusing on his strengths and embracing self-compassion, Paul built a reservoir of resilience. Challenges no longer loomed as insurmountable obstacles but became opportunities for growth. The tightness in his chest eased, replaced by a quiet confidence. He started to sleep better, laugh more, and approach his work with renewed enthusiasm.

Paul's journey was a winding road of self-discovery. He learned that inner love isn't about ignoring flaws or past mistakes; it's about accepting oneself wholly and striving for growth. By changing the way, he saw himself, he changed his world.

His story is a powerful reminder that our lives are not solely defined by our failures but by the narratives we choose to embrace. If you find yourself overwhelmed by setbacks, take a moment to pause and reflect. Acknowledge your strengths, no matter how overshadowed they may feel. Celebrate your achievements, both big and small. Remember that your worth isn't determined by what hasn't gone right but by the resilience, creativity, and compassion you bring to each new day.

Embrace inner love. Let it be the foundation upon which you build your resilience. Allow it to shift your perspective, turning challenges into steppingstones rather than stumbling blocks. Just like Paul, you have the power to rewrite your story, transforming moments of doubt into a journey toward a more fulfilling and confident life.

Remember, the most significant change begins within. By choosing to see yourself through a lens of kindness and strength, you open the door to endless possibilities. Your past does not define your future—you do. In chapter 5 you will engage in a loving-kindness exercise to deepen your self-compassion and inner peace.

Benefits of Inner love
Calming inner love is a transformative practice that fosters a positive mindset, empowering you to navigate life's challenges with confidence and resilience. By embracing inner love, you affirm your inherent worth and capabilities, creating a strong foundation to handle stress, overcome obstacles, and bounce back from setbacks with ease.

The benefits of inner love are profound and far-reaching; they are stated below.

1. **Resilience:** Inner love helps you develop a growth mindset, allowing you to reframe challenges as opportunities for growth and learning.
2. **Stress Management:** By affirming your worth, you're better equipped to cope with stress, reducing the risk of burnout and emotional exhaustion.
3. **Mental Well-being:** Studies demonstrate that individuals who practice Inner love are less likely to experience anxiety and depression, leading to improved overall mental health.
4. **Increased Confidence:** Inner love encourages self-acceptance, helping you develop a positive self-image and unshakeable confidence in your abilities.
5. **Improved Relationships:** When you love yourself, you're more likely to form healthy, fulfilling relationships built on mutual respect and trust.
6. **Enhanced Self-Awareness:** Inner love nurtures introspection, allowing you to deeply understand your values, passions, and goals—ultimately guiding you toward a more authentic and purpose-driven life. Personally, I've found that after just 30 minutes of mindful activities like running or meditation, my mind naturally shifts into a creative state, often bringing forth new insights and wisdom. As Eckhart Tolle wisely said, "Stillness is where creativity and solutions to problems are found."

CHAPTER 2

BARRIERS TO INNER LOVE

Common Obstacle

A common obstacle is a habitual challenge or obstructions that commonly delay progress or success across various situations or contexts. It often manifests in the form of practical difficulties, psychological barriers, or resource limitations that individuals or groups encounter while pursuing goals. Such obstacles can stem from internal factors, like lack of motivation or skills, or assumed external factors, such as economic constraints or environmental conditions, and can significantly affect the ability to achieve desired outcomes or maintain momentum.

1. Negative Self-Talk

There's a voice inside all of us, often referred to as our inner dialogue—a voice that lurks in the shadows, waiting for the perfect moment to strike. It knows exactly where to aim to hurt us the most. It whispers in quiet moments when we're alone with our thoughts, wielding words like weapons. These words can leave psychological scars, manifesting as anxiety or depression: "No one likes you," "You'll never succeed," "You're not good enough."

This voice emerges when you're on the brink of something new, something significant, pulling you back with doubts and fears that feel heavier than mountains. It often ties directly to our perceived self-image, shaped by past experiences, particularly those from childhood. It might whisper, "Nobody has ever done it in your family," "What makes you think you'll succeed? Don't waste your time," or even, "You might succeed, but then people will envy you." And just as you're about to face another challenge, it delivers its final blow: "Why even try?" This is the voice of negative self-talk—a relentless, nagging presence that knows how to turn every stumble into a full-blown fall, every mistake into a monumental failure. For years, I let that voice dictate my life. I believed it was the voice of reason, a guide to keep me humble and cautious, protecting me from disappointment. But in reality, all it ever did was keep me small, afraid to reach for what was already within me.

The truth is, negative self-talk is not the voice of truth—it's the voice of fear in disguise, an echo from the past experiences and imagined failures that has no rightful place in our present or future. It is the ghost of old wounds, old stories, self-image and long-held beliefs that do not serve the person we are becoming. Breaking free from this inner critic isn't about silencing it or battling it into submission. It's about recognizing it for what it truly is: a scared, wounded part of you that needs compassion, not control. It's the voice of your inner child, trying to protect you in the only way it knows how—by building walls where there should be bridges.

The next time this voice rises and starts its familiar monologue, take a moment to pause. Breathe deeply and feel the steadiness of your breath, the rhythm of life flowing through you. Ask yourself, "Is this really true? Or is this just fear speaking?" If you can vividly remember the entire dialogue, write it down on a piece of paper and ask yourself, "is this voice in me or on paper" then listen and allow yourself to sit with it for a while. Thank it for trying to keep you safe but remind it gently that you're ready for something different now. Because you don't have to be defined by fear anymore. You have the power to write a new narrative—one where you are not only capable but also deserving, one where you are worthy and enough just as you are.

Imagine the liberation that comes from rewriting the script. See yourself standing at the threshold of a new beginning, and instead of hearing "You can't," you hear a different voice, one that says, "You can. And you will." And suddenly, the world around you seems a little less intimidating, a little more filled with possibility. This is the power of choosing a new story, one where that inner critic transforms from a harsh judge to a quiet reminder of how far you've come.

But how do you turn that inner critic into a source of strength? How do you change those old, tired narratives that have held you back for so long? You might wonder. Later in this chapter, we will embark on a powerful exercise— Steps to Overcoming Negative Self-Talk Journal—a journey deep into your own-awareness. Here, you'll learn how to catch those negative thoughts as they arise, challenge them, and replace them with words that uplift and empower you. You will uncover the hidden truths within you that have always been there, waiting for a voice and as you do, you'll begin to see that this journey isn't just about quieting a critic; it's about finding the courage to be your own greatest advocate. Because you are not your fears—you are the love, resilience, and possibility that have been waiting to break free. Let's dive into this transformative work together and rewrite the story of who you are meant to be.

Breaking Free from the Inner Critic

The morning sun poured through the sheer curtains of Sarah's apartment, casting a soft glow on the scattered papers and half-empty coffee cups that littered her desk. She sat hunched over her laptop, eyes darting over the email she had just received. Another project revision requested by her boss.

"How could I have missed that?" she muttered, her heart sinking. A familiar voice echoed in her mind, sharp and unforgiving. "You're so stupid. You'll never get anything right." The words stung, and she felt tears welling up.

She slammed the laptop shut and buried her face in her hands. "Why am I like this?" she thought. "Why can't I be competent like everyone else?" The city buzzed outside, but inside, Sarah was trapped in a spiral of self-doubt.

Later that day, she walked aimlessly through the park, leaves crunching under her feet. Children laughed in the distance, and dogs chased after frisbees, oblivious to her inner turmoil. She sat on a bench and watched a little girl learning to ride a bike. The child wobbled and fell, scraping her knee. Before the tears could fall, her mother rushed to her side, offering encouragement.

"It's okay, sweetie. Everyone falls when they're learning. Try again—you're doing great!"

Sarah felt a pang in her chest. "Why can't I be that gentle with myself?" she wondered. The mother's words echoed in her mind as she made her way home, resonating with a truth she had long forgotten.

That evening, she stood in front of her mirror, taking a long look at herself. Her eyes were tired, but there was a glimmer of determination. "Enough is enough," she whispered. "I can't keep tearing myself down."

She sat cross-legged on her bed, pulling out a notebook. On the right side of the page, she wrote down every harsh thought that plagued her: Staring at the words, she felt a surge of defiance. On the left side she began to counter them:

"You're useless."	"I have overcome challenges before."
"You'll never succeed."	"I am learning and growing."
"You're a failure."	"I am capable of success."

The next morning, Sarah woke up to the sound of birds chirping. For the first time in a long while, she didn't feel the weight of dread pressing down on her. As she prepared her breakfast, she accidentally dropped a plate, watching it shatter on the floor.

She braced herself for the onslaught of self-criticism. The sharp reprimand was on the tip of her tongue when the memory of the mother in the park flashed in her mind.

"It's okay... Everyone falls when they're learning."

She took a deep breath. "It's just a plate. Accidents happen," she told herself gently, echoing the mother's comforting tone. A small smile tugged at her lips. "I'm still learning to be kind to myself."

"Progress," she thought, as she swept up the broken pieces. The simple act of self-compassion felt liberating, a tiny victory over the harsh critic inside her.

Weeks passed, and each day Sarah made a conscious effort to challenge the negativity. When she received feedback at work, she viewed it as an opportunity to improve rather than a confirmation of her inadequacy. "I can handle this," she would say. "I'm getting better every day."

One afternoon, her friend Maya noticed the change. "You seem different lately, more confident," Maya remarked over coffee.

Sarah smiled thoughtfully. "I've started being kinder to myself," she admitted. "It's amazing how much lighter I feel."

Her inner dialogue had shifted from a harsh critic to a supportive ally. The mistakes she made were no longer catastrophes but steppingstones. She began to embrace her journey, imperfections and all.

Standing on her balcony one evening, watching the sunset paint the sky with hues of orange and pink, Sarah felt a deep sense of peace. "I'm proud of how far I've come," she thought. "I am worthy of love and respect—especially from myself."

Sarah's transformation illuminates a powerful truth: the most significant battles are often within us, but so are the most profound victories. Negative self-talk doesn't have to control your life. Like Sarah, you have the strength to confront and change those destructive thoughts.

As you proceed in the pages of Nurturing inner love, we will delve deeper into overcoming negative self-talk and transforming them into words of affirmation. You'll learn practical steps to recognize and challenge the critical voice inside of you, replacing it with compassionate and empowering messages.

By actively participating in this exercise, you'll find that the voice that once held you back can become a powerful force propelling you forward. Embrace the journey toward self-awareness and watch as it transforms not just your inner world, but every aspect of your life.

2. Past Traumas

We all carry scars—some etched across our skin, others buried deep within the chambers of our hearts. These scars tell stories of where we've been wounded, where life has cut us to the bone and left us gasping for air. They are the silent echoes of pain, moments when the world seemed to shatter around us, leaving behind fragments we've tried to piece together ever since. But if you look closely, those scars are also proof of where we've healed, where we've risen from the ashes, forged stronger by the fires that sought to destroy us. They are marks not of defeat, but of resilience. The past does not define you—it is a wise teacher, a map of where you've been that can guide you to where you are meant to go. If you let it, it can transform you in ways you never thought possible.

Healing from past traumas is not about forgetting the pain or erasing it from memory; it's about finding the courage to face it, to sit with it, and to whisper to your wounds, "You do not control me. I will not be your prisoner. Instead, I will use you to become stronger, wiser, and more compassionate." Picture yourself standing tall, like a tree battered by storms, its bark scarred but roots deepened, branches reaching ever higher toward the light. Every time you confront your pain, you dig your roots deeper, grounding yourself in the truth that you are not what happened to you—you are what you choose to become.

Remember the story of overcoming a bad day in Chapter One, where I shared the ending of a relationship with the words, "I think this relationship is going nowhere, I need more time and space to work on myself." At that moment, those words felt like a sudden and devastating blow, shattering everything familiar and casting me into a sea of deep uncertainty.

Looking back now, I see how that experience became a catalyst for one of the most profound transformations of my life. Not because I wanted the relationship to end, but because of the wisdom that arose in its absence. As Less Brown famously says, "we live life looking forward but understand it looking backwards." And this perfectly captures the clarity I found through reflection.

True transformation, I realized, isn't something you can force or control. Like the seasons changing or a flower slowly unfurling its petals, so is transformation must unfold naturally. When we try to force it, we risk shutting ourselves off from the very insights our soul is waiting to reveal.

Transformation demands deep, unwavering awareness—a willingness to face the unknown and the courage to confront your inner shadows. It is like standing before a blank canvas and daring to paint your life with the colors of your deepest truths. You begin to understand that every heartache, every joy, every goodbye, and every hello is a brushstroke shaping the masterpiece of who you are becoming.

To truly grasp which moments define you, you must walk the winding path of self-awareness. You must learn to sit quietly with your past—not as a judge, but as a curious traveler, reflecting on each fork in the road, each choice, each turning point. Only by journeying with an open heart and clear eyes can you start to see which stories are worth sharing—those rare gems that hold the power to inspire, uplift, and awaken the human spirit.

When I finally embraced this path of self-reflection, my life began to shift. My experiences were no longer a series of disconnected events; they transformed into a rich mosaic woven with purpose and meaning. I started to see which experiences carried the deepest lessons. These are the stories I now offer—not just as anecdotes, but as catalysts for elevating consciousness, healing wounds, and reminding us all of the transformative power of love and awareness.

Ralph Waldo Emerson once wrote in his essay Self-Reliance, "What I must do is all that concerns me, not what the people think." This powerful statement captures the essence of true healing. It reminds us that our journey is uniquely our own, not defined by the expectations or judgments of others, but by our ability to rise and reclaim our power. Emerson believed in the sovereignty of the self, in trusting one's inner voice above all others. Isn't that what healing truly requires? To trust yourself enough to walk through the flames of your past, to see the strength within your scars, and to emerge, not as the person you once were, but as the person you were always meant to be.

The path to healing is not a straight line; it's a labyrinth of twists and turns, dark nights, and moments of breathtaking clarity. Some days, it feels like stepping out of a dense fog, each step heavier than the last, but still moving forward, still finding your way. Other days, it feels like you've been pulled back into the darkness, like every step forward has been undone. But remember this: even in those moments of despair, even when it feels like you're back at the beginning, you are not. You are carrying with you all the strength, all the lessons, all the growth from each step you've already taken. Your scars have already made you stronger, even when you can't see it.

There will be days when the ghosts of your past rise up, when the memories flood in like a tidal wave, and you feel yourself being pulled under. They haunt you with flashbacks, compel you to avoid the places, the faces, the moments that trigger those old wounds. But know this: you have the power to rewrite the narrative, to walk back into those shadows with the light of your own resilience burning brightly. Healing isn't about banishing the darkness; it's about becoming the kind of person who can hold both the dark and the light, who can stand in the middle of the storm and say, "I am still here. I am still standing."

As Emerson also said, "To be yourself in a world that is constantly trying to make you something else is the greatest accomplishment." To face your past, to embrace your scars, and to stand firm in your truth—that is self-reliance. That is healing. Give yourself grace. Be gentle with your heart as it unravels and re-knits itself, thread by thread. Know that healing is not a race; it is a sacred journey that unfolds in its own time. Be patient with yourself on the days when it feels like the weight of your past is too heavy to bear. Remember that even in your quietest moments, when progress seems invisible, the very act of choosing to heal is a revolutionary act of courage.

As you move through this journey of self-awareness, remember scars do not make you weak—they make you human. They make you whole. They are the marks of a life lived deeply, of a heart that has known both agony and triumph. Wear them with pride. They are the proof that, no matter what tried to break you, you chose to heal, to rise, to love again. You are a testament to what it means to be beautifully, powerfully, unbreakably human. As Emerson would remind us, "Trust thyself: every heart vibrates to that iron string."

Later in this chapter, you will be invited to reflect on the scars you carry, both seen and unseen. What stories do they tell? What strength have they given you? Begin to see them not as marks of what broke you but as symbols of what you've overcome. Share your journey with others. Be the light that shows someone else that healing is possible, that rising from the ashes is not just a dream but a reality. Trust yourself, honor your journey, and remember—you are not alone in this path of becoming. Embrace your scars and let them guide you to the wholeness you seek.

Healing the Wounds That Hold You Back

John's story is a testament to this struggle. As a child, he endured relentless bullying, which left him with a lingering sense of unworthiness that followed him into adulthood. No matter what he achieved, that little voice in his head whispered that it wasn't enough, that he wasn't enough. This trauma infiltrated his relationships, driving him to constantly seek validation from others, as if their approval could fill the void that the bullying had carved out in his heart.

But validation from others was never enough. John realized that if he wanted to truly heal, he needed to face the trauma head-on. Through therapy, he began to unravel the pain that had been tightly wound around his self-esteem for so long. Each therapy session was like peeling back layers of hurt, fear, and self-doubt, revealing the raw wounds that needed to heal.

John also turned to reflective journaling, a practice that allowed him to confront his past with honesty and courage. Writing down his thoughts and emotions, he began to see patterns in his behavior—how the child who was bullied had grown into an adult who doubted his own worth. But through this process, something extraordinary happened: John started to rewrite his story. He realized that he was not defined by his past, but by how he chose to respond to it.

As he worked through his trauma, John began to build a healthier relationship with himself. He learned to give himself the validation and compassion he had always sought from others. Slowly, the chains of his past loosened, and he found a new sense of harmony—both within himself and in his relationships with others.

John's journey reminds us that healing from past trauma is not only possible but essential for cultivating inner love. It's a path that requires immense courage and patience, but it leads to a place of profound peace and self-acceptance. If you're struggling with the weight of past traumas, take heart in knowing that healing is within your reach. Start by acknowledging the impact these experiences have had on your life and then take deliberate steps toward healing—whether through therapy, journaling, or other means of self-reflection.

Remember, your past does not define you. You have the power to heal, to build a relationship with yourself that is based on love, compassion, and respect. As you begin this journey, you'll discover that inner love is not just about accepting who you are today, but about healing the wounds of yesterday to create a brighter, more fulfilling tomorrow. Take that first step, and let your story be one of resilience, growth, and the transformative power of inner love.

3. Societal Pressures

Societal pressures can be relentless, dictating unrealistic standards of success, beauty, and behavior. We're constantly bombarded by images and messages that tell us we must look a certain way, achieve certain milestones, and behave in ways that are often impossible to sustain. This barrage, amplified by media and social interactions, can leave us feeling inadequate, forever chasing an elusive ideal, and desperate to "measure up."

Navigating Social Expectations at a Wedding

One day, I attended my friend's wedding—a dazzling celebration filled with beautiful decorations and friends and family dressed to the nines. I felt perfectly attired for the occasion, excited to be part of an event that many dream of but few experience—a rare, unforgettable day. A small, hopeful thought crossed my mind: Maybe I will attract one of the attendees here to be my partner.

As the Master of Ceremonies introduced the bride and groom, the reception continued with captivating entertainment that demanded everyone's attention. The MC sprinkled jokes throughout the evening, eliciting laughter, cheers, and occasional puzzled looks. Most of his humor was lighthearted, but one joke stood out—it was directed at me.

He said, "Some of you are here and wish it was your turn, like my friend Val. You're overdue, and you have all the qualities and attributes to make a great marriage." His words struck me like lightning. For a moment, I stared blankly at my drink, my body suddenly tense, as cold as ice. The timing was uncanny; it was as if the universe had spoken, aligning perfectly with my earlier thoughts. His words echoed what I had been thinking just moments before, and perhaps because of that, they didn't sting as much. I thought, "The universe has spoken."

A close friend tapped me on the back and whispered, "People are staring at you." As I regained my composure, another friend leaned in and murmured, "That wasn't appropriate. He shouldn't have mentioned your personal life here." I could feel the eyes on me and a mix of emotions swirling inside—embarrassment, surprise, maybe even a bit of frustration. But I've always tried to stay present and appreciate each moment. I took a deep breath and decided not to take it personally. After all, it was just a joke, and perhaps there was some truth in his words. And maybe, because his words had mirrored my own secret hope, they didn't sting as much.

This experience reminded me that we often can't control society's expectations or how they are voiced. Our journeys are deeply personal, requiring patience, persistence, and consistent effort. I reminded myself to celebrate each moment and embrace my unique path. Sometimes, others' expectations and comments become part of our journey, but we shouldn't let them weigh too heavily on our hearts.

Living in the moment empowers us to navigate situations thoughtfully. When faced with unexpected scenarios, first assess whether a comment or expectation deserves your energy. If it doesn't, embrace it as part of your journey and move forward. Instead of feeling pressured, seek insight from those who have expectations of you—they might hold the key to fulfilling what's expected.

I remember an incident involving my friend Martin, a human resource professional. At a party we both attended, Martin made a joke about one of his employees. Unfortunately, the employee took the joke personally. The next day, he didn't show up for work, claiming his absence was meant to make Martin "feel the void." That moment showed me how misunderstandings can escalate when emotions take over and reactions become impulsive.

Now, imagine yourself in a similar situation. How would you choose to respond? Would you let the weight of a moment dictate your actions, or would you pause, reflect, and decide with clarity? These choices matter, not just for the outcome but for how they shape your own journey.

Such experiences remind all of us to cherish each moment, stay true to our paths, and recognize that others' views are just fragments of a much larger, personal story. The universe often speaks to us through these situations, inviting us to listen and respond with wisdom, grace, and emotional maturity.

Reclaiming Your Authentic Self

Julie's story is one many of us can relate to. She felt immense pressure to maintain a "perfect" image on social media. Every post, every photo, was meticulously crafted to portray an ideal life. She would spend hours editing pictures, choosing the right filters, and crafting captions that made everything seem flawless. From the outside, it looked like she had it all together—a life filled with beauty, success, and happiness. But behind the screen, the reality was starkly different.

The constant pressure to live up to this manufactured image took a heavy toll. Julie felt disconnected from her true self, consumed by the need to maintain an illusion that didn't reflect her real life. The endless pursuit of perfection led to burnout, anxiety, and a deep sense of emptiness. Her life had become a performance, and she was losing herself in the process.

One day, Julie made a courageous decision. She stepped back from social media, taking a break from the endless cycle of comparison and validation. At first, it felt as though she was disappearing from a world where she had invested so much of herself. However, as the noise quieted, something beautiful began to happen—Julie started to reconnect with her authentic self.

It reminds me of a conversation with a friend who once declared, "I'm going to delete my social media accounts for two years and come back as an influencer." Though I doubted he ever followed through, the sentiment stuck with me. It underscored the allure of stepping away to return transformed.

Without the pressure to portray a perfect life, Julie redirected her energy to her real-life relationships. She spent meaningful time with loved ones, engaged in heartfelt conversations, and rediscovered passions that had been buried under the weight of societal expectations. In doing so, she realized that the connections she craved couldn't be found through likes or followers but through genuine interactions and self-acceptance.

As Julie reconnected with her true self, she found a new kind of peace—one that wasn't dependent on external validation or the approval of others. She embraced her imperfections, understanding that they were what made her unique and beautiful. By stepping back from societal pressures, she discovered that her worth wasn't defined by how she appeared to others, but by the authenticity with which she lived her life.

Julie's journey is a powerful reminder that the path to inner love begins with rejecting the unrealistic standards society imposes on us. If you're feeling overwhelmed by the pressure to "measure up," take a moment to step back and reassess. Ask yourself: Who am I trying to impress? What am I sacrificing in this pursuit of perfection? And most importantly, what would it feel like to live authentically, true to who you really are?

You have the power to reclaim your life from societal pressures. It begins with reconnecting with yourself, valuing your real-life relationships, and embracing the imperfect, beautiful reality of who you are. Step away from the filters, the edits, and the need to perform. You don't have to go to the extreme of deleting your social media accounts, but you can consciously navigate social media with positive intentions. As the saying goes, the very things we avoid are often the very things that liberate us. Embrace your true self, and you'll discover that the love and acceptance you've been seeking have been within you all along.

4. Fear of Vulnerability

The fear of vulnerability is a powerful force, rooted in the deep-seated worry that revealing your true self will lead to rejection or judgment. It's a fear that keeps us guarded, hiding behind walls of stoicism or perfection, and it robs us of the chance to form deep, meaningful connections. Most tragically, it keeps us from fully embracing inner love, because we never let ourselves be truly seen—not by others, and not even by ourselves.

Embracing the Power of Authenticity

Francis knew this fear all too well. For years, he masked his emotions behind a facade of strength, believing that any sign of vulnerability would make him seem weak. He kept his struggles hidden, convinced that revealing them would diminish his worth. But despite his efforts to appear invulnerable, an invisible barrier separated him from the world. Even among friends, he felt isolated—like no one truly knew him.

I understand this struggle because I, too, have walked that path. I used to believe that seeking help was a sign of weakness, that relying on others meant exposing my flaws. So, I chose to carry my burdens alone, convinced that independence was the only way to prove my strength. But no matter how much I tried to handle everything on my own, something always felt missing. The isolation became suffocating, and eventually, the weight of self-reliance took its toll—leading to moments of anxiety, even depression.

Francis reached that breaking point as well. "One day, the weight of carrying my burdens alone became too much to bear," he admitted. "In a moment of quiet desperation, I made a decision that changed my life—I opened up to a close friend about my struggles."

He braced himself for judgment, maybe even pity. But instead, he was met with something unexpected: understanding and support. His friend didn't see him as weak; he saw him as human. And in that moment, Francis realized something profound—vulnerability wasn't a weakness; it was a bridge to deeper connection.

This revelation transformed him. By allowing himself to be seen—flaws and all—Francis discovered that true strength lies in authenticity. The walls he had built for protection had only kept him from what he craved most—genuine, meaningful relationships. As he let them crumble, his connections with others grew stronger, more honest, and more fulfilling.

Francis's journey, like my own, is a testament to the power of vulnerability. We often fear that exposing our struggles will push people away, but in reality, it does the opposite—it draws in those who truly care.

If you're struggling with the fear of vulnerability, consider this: What would it feel like to be truly seen and accepted—not despite your flaws, but because of them? What would it mean to show up in your relationships as your authentic self, without the masks, without the fear?

Take a step toward vulnerability today. Open up, even if it feels uncomfortable. Share a part of yourself that you've kept hidden and see what happens. You might be surprised to find that what you feared would push people away actually draws them closer. Vulnerability is the key to unlocking the deep, meaningful connections we all yearn for.

Don't let fear hold you back—embrace your true self and let the world see the beauty of your authenticity.

2.1 The Bitter Truth Personal story

One day, a friend invited me to his son's birthday party. Naturally, I couldn't resist the allure of free cake, so I eagerly joined the celebration. As we were catching up, my friend casually asked, "So, how's your girlfriend?" I replied, "Things didn't work out, and we went our separate ways." Without missing a beat, he responded with a bluntness that caught me off guard: "Well, you know, the problem is you don't look all that attractive."

Ouch. His words hit me like a ton of bricks, but I kept my cool, masking the sting with a smile. I continued with the party, pretending his remark hadn't cut as deep as a bad haircut on picture day.

That night, though, as I lay in bed, his comment replayed in my mind. It hurt, no doubt about it, but it also stirred something within me. I realized that his brutal honesty, though harsh, had given me a wake-up call. I was just beginning my journey of self-care, trying to improve my physique and overall well-being, and his words, as bitter as they were, resonated deeply. Instead of wallowing in self-pity, I found a surprising source of motivation to take even better care of myself.

Looking back, I can't help but laugh at the absurdity of the situation. But more importantly, I recognize the truth in it—sometimes, the most unexpected, even painful comments can ignite the greatest changes in your life. They force you to confront the uncomfortable truths you'd rather ignore and, in doing so, propel you toward growth.

If you've ever been on the receiving end of a harsh truth, know this: You have the power to turn it into fuel for your self-awareness journey. Let those words, no matter how cutting, be the spark that drives you to become the best version of yourself. Embrace the discomfort, use it as motivation, and remember that every challenge, even one wrapped in bitter honesty, is an opportunity to grow stronger, wiser, and more resilient.

2.2 Thought Journal Exercise

This activity is designed to help you become more aware of your thoughts—especially negative ones or self-criticisms. By writing them down, you can start to identify recurring patterns and triggers. This is the first step toward changing those thought patterns and fostering a more positive, self-compassionate mindset.

Imagine gaining deeper insight into the thoughts that shape your emotions and behaviors. This awareness empowers you to challenge and transform negative thoughts, leading to enhanced mental well-being, greater inner love, and personal growth. Research shows that practicing inner love has significant mental health benefits. For example, Neff and Germer (2013) found that practicing self-compassion, a core aspect of Self-love, is associated with lower levels of anxiety and depression.

Steps to Overcoming Negative Self-Talk Journal
Step 1: Prepare Your Journal

Choose a notebook or digital document for your thought Journal. Personalize it to make it more inviting and comfortable.

Step 2: Set a Daily Routine

Make journaling a daily habit by capturing your thoughts as they arise. Keep your journal easily accessible so you can jot down insights throughout the day. Personally, I use the Voice Memo app on my Apple iPhone to record my thoughts as they come.

I've noticed that my most intuitive ideas often emerge when I'm engaged with thought-provoking content, such as controversial podcasts or videos, or when reflecting on an undesirable outcome from a situation. Interestingly, the best possible answers tend to surface when I'm exercising, showering, or meditating—moments when my mind is free and open to deeper insights.

To maintain a balanced mindset, I consciously focus on the positive aspects of my well-being. By doing so, I seamlessly transform negative thoughts into creative and constructive perspectives, allowing challenges to become opportunities for growth and innovation.

Step 3: Capture Your Thoughts

Description

1. **Date and Time:** Write the date and time of each entry.
2. **Thought:** Describe the negative thought or self-criticism. What were you thinking? What triggered it?
3. **Context:** Describe the situation or context in which the thought occurred. Were you at work? Talking to a friend? Alone at home?
4. **Emotion:** Write down how the thought made you feel. Anxious? Sad? Frustrated?
5. **Reflection:** Briefly reflect on why you might have had this thought. Is it a recurring theme? What might have triggered it?

Example Templates for Journaling

Date	Time	Thought	Context	Emotion	Reflection
July 5, 2099	3:00 PM	"I can't do anything right"	After making a mistake at work	Frustrated, Disappointed	I often feel this way After In stakes. This might be tied to a fear of judgment and perfectionism.

Fill in Template

Date	Time	Thought	Context	Emotion	Reflection

Step 4: Identify Patterns and Triggers

After a week or two of consistent journaling, take a step back and review your entries. This reflection will help you:

   1. Identify patterns in your thoughts

2. Recognize common triggers
3. Ask yourself these questions
4. Are there specific situations that frequently lead to negative thoughts?
5. Are certain people or environments associated with self-criticism?
6. Do specific types of negative thoughts recur?

By reviewing your journal entries, you'll gain valuable insight into your thought patterns and triggers, allowing you to recognize and address them more effectively. As you continue, you'll be introduced to exercises designed to help you transform negative thoughts into positivity.

Activity: Pattern and Trigger Analysis
1. **Review Entries**: Read through your journal entries.
2. **Highlight Patterns:** Use a highlighter or make notes to identify recurring themes and triggers.
3. **Summarize Findings:** Write a summary of your findings. What are the most common negative thoughts? What triggers them?

Example Analysis

Common Thoughts: "I can't do anything right," "I'm not good enough."
Triggers: Work presentations, social gatherings, comparing myself to others on social media.
Summary: I notice that I often feel inadequate in professional and social settings, particularly when I make mistakes or compare myself to others.

Your Analysis

Common Thoughts: "_____"
Triggers: "_____"
Summary: "_____"

Step 5: Challenge and transform Negative Thoughts into Positive

Once you've identified negative self-talk, the next step is to challenge it. Ask yourself, "Is this thought true? Is it helpful? Would I say this to a friend?" More often than not, these thoughts are exaggerated or unfounded. Reframe them with positive affirmations that reflect your true worth and take time to meditate on them until they become ingrained in your mindset.

Exercise transformation

1. **Identify a Negative Thought:** Choose a recurring negative thought from your journal.
2. **Question the Thought:** Ask yourself:

Is this thought true?

What evidence do I have?

Is this thought helpful?

How does it make me feel?

Would I say this to a friend?

How would I respond if a friend said this about themselves?

3. **Transform the Thought:** Find a more positive or balanced perspective. For example:

Negative Thought: "I can't do anything right."

Transformed Thought: "I made a mistake, but I can learn from it and improve."

Example Entry

Negative Thought: "I'm not good enough."

Question: Is this thought true? No, I have many accomplishments and strengths. Is this thought helpful? No, it makes me feel discouraged. Would I say this to a friend? No, I would remind them of their worth.

Transformed Thought: "I have strengths and areas for growth.
I am doing my best and that's enough."

Your Entry:

Negative Thought:"_____"

Question: "_____"

Transformed Thought:"_____"

_____

Step 6: Reflect and Practice Self-Compassion

Review your progress weekly.

Write down any positive changes or insights.

_____

_____

_____

Practice self-compassion:

Acknowledge your efforts and encourage yourself to keep going. The key to progress lies in understanding why you engage in this practice. This deeper purpose will serve as your motivation, especially on days when it feels like you're not making progress. Remember, every step—no matter how small—moves you forward on your journey of growth.

Weekly Reflection Example

Date: July 1, 2099

Weekly Reflection: This week, I noticed I'm becoming more aware of my negative thoughts. I successfully transformed "I can't do anything right" to "I made a mistake, but I can learn from it." I feel more hopeful and less critical of myself.

Self-Compassion Note: "I'm proud of myself for taking steps to change my thought patterns. It's okay to have setbacks, and I am doing my best. I am worthy of love and compassion."

Sophia's Journey to Self-Compassion

Meet Sophia, a bright and capable individual who was, unfortunately, her own worst critic. Inside her mind lived a relentless voice, one that constantly berated her for not meeting impossible standards of "perfection." Every mistake was magnified, every flaw scrutinized, and every achievement downplayed. Her self-criticism was suffocating, leaving her feeling inadequate and undeserving of success or happiness.

Sophia's habit of comparing herself to others only made things worse. She'd scroll through social media, feeling inferior to the curated highlight reels of her peers. At social gatherings, she was convinced everyone else was more intelligent, more charming, and more successful. This constant comparison drained her spirit and kept her locked in a cycle of self-doubt.

One day, in a moment of desperation for change, Sophia stumbled upon a thought-journaling technique. She decided to give it a try, committing to writing down every thought, no matter how painful or embarrassing, for a week. The exercise was more revealing than she could have imagined.

As Sophia reviewed her journal entries, she was stunned by the harshness of her inner dialogue. She saw clearly how she'd been bullying herself, perpetuating a cycle of fear and negativity. But amid this realization, she also saw a glimmer of hope—an opportunity to change. With this newfound awareness, Sophia began to challenge her negative thoughts. She asked herself: "Is this thought really true?" "Is there another way to look at this situation?" "What would I say to a friend facing the same challenges?"

Little by little, Sophia started to replace her critical inner voice with positive affirmations. She shifted her focus from her perceived flaws to her genuine strengths, from her mistakes to her resilience, and from her doubts to her accomplishments. She began to see herself through a kinder, more compassionate lens.

As the weeks turned into months, Sophia noticed a profound transformation in her mindset. She felt more confident, more self-assured, and, most importantly, at peace with who she was. She realized that she didn't need to be perfect to be worthy—she was enough, just as she was.

Sophia's story is a powerful reminder that we don't have to be prisoners of our negative thoughts. If you find yourself caught in a cycle of self-criticism, take a page from Sophia's book: confront those thoughts, challenge them, and replace them with affirmations that reflect your true value. You have the power to rewrite your inner dialogue and transform your relationship with yourself.

Start today. Grab a journal, write down your thoughts, and face them head-on. You might be surprised at the strength and compassion you uncover within yourself. Remember, the journey to inner love isn't about achieving perfection—it's about embracing who you are, flaws and all, and knowing that you are enough. Let Sophia's journey inspire you to take action and start your own path to self-compassion and inner peace.

Addressing Past Traumas

Recommendations for Professional Help and Self-Care Techniques

i. Seek Professional Help (Therapy and Counseling)

If you find that past traumas are significantly impacting your daily life, seeking professional help is crucial. Therapists and counselors are trained to help you process and heal from harrowing experiences. Various therapeutic approaches, such as Cognitive Behavioral Therapy (CBT), Eye Movement Desensitization and Reprocessing (EMDR), and trauma-informed therapy, can be beneficial.

ii. Support Groups

Joining a support group can provide a sense of community and understanding. Sharing your experiences with others who have faced similar challenges can be incredibly healing and empowering.

iii. Hotlines and Crisis Resources

In times of acute distress, hotlines and crisis resources can provide immediate support. Don't hesitate to reach out if you need urgent help.

2. Self-Care Techniques (Mindfulness and Meditation)

Practicing mindfulness and meditation can help you stay grounded and present. These techniques can reduce anxiety and improve emotional regulation. Apps like Headspace and Calm offer guided meditations specifically designed for trauma recovery.

i. **Journaling:** Writing about your experiences can be a powerful way to process and release emotions. Use your journal to explore your thoughts and feelings, and to track your progress over time.
ii. **Physical Activity:** Engaging in regular physical activity can help reduce stress and improve mood. Activities like yoga, walking, and swimming are particularly beneficial for trauma recovery.
iii. **Creative Expression:** Art, music, and dance can be therapeutic outlets for expressing and processing emotions. Find a creative activity that resonates with you and incorporate it into your self-care routine.

Stories of Personal Recovery and Resilience
Jane's Journey to Healing

Jane's childhood was marked by significant trauma, leaving her feeling unworthy and disconnected from herself and the world around her. The weight of her past cast long shadows over her present, filling her with self-doubt and a deep sense of emptiness. For years, Jane carried this burden alone, convinced that she was unworthy of love and belonging.

One day, Jane decided she couldn't keep living in the shadows of her pain. She took a brave step and sought therapy, determined to confront the wounds that had shaped her life. In therapy, she learned to face her past with courage and compassion. Through EMDR therapy, she began to process the traumatic memories that had kept her trapped. Each session was like peeling back layers of hurt and fear, revealing parts of herself she had long buried.

Journaling became another lifeline, a space where Jane could pour out her unspoken thoughts and emotions. On the page, she gave voice to her pain, her anger, and her hopes, slowly untangling the threads of her past. Mindfulness practices helped her stay grounded in the present, teaching her to breathe through the discomfort and embrace her journey without judgment.

As Jane navigated this path of healing, she rediscovered a forgotten passion: painting. With every brushstroke, she found a new way to express the emotions she couldn't put into words. Her canvases became a testament to her resilience, each one capturing the raw, beautiful complexity of her inner world. Painting wasn't just an escape—it was a reclamation of her voice, a celebration of her journey toward wholeness.

Over time, Jane's self-worth began to blossom. The chains of her past loosened, and she started to see herself not through the lens of her trauma, but through the eyes of compassion and strength. She built resilience, layer by layer, and began to live a life that felt more connected, more authentic, and more her own.

Jane's journey is a powerful reminder that healing is possible, no matter how deep the wounds. If you've been carrying the weight of your past, know that you have the power to change your story. Seek the support you need, whether through therapy, journaling, or creative expression. Take the courageous steps toward your own healing and allow yourself the grace to feel and grow.

Remember, you are not defined by what has happened to you, but by how you choose to rise from it. Let Jane's story inspire you to embrace your journey, knowing that on the other side of pain lies a life of connection, self-worth, and the freedom to be exactly who you are. Take that first step—your healing begins with the decision to honor yourself and your journey.

How to Identify and Acknowledge Barriers to Inner Love

❖ **Self-Awareness:** The first step in overcoming these barriers is to become aware of them. You can't fix what you don't acknowledge. Start by paying attention to your thoughts and feelings. Notice when you engage in negative self-talk or when past traumas resurface. Recognize the societal pressures or experiences that influence your self-perception.

Self-Assessment Quiz: Identifying Barriers to Inner Love

1. Do you often find yourself thinking negative thoughts about yourself?

a) Yes

b) No

Do past experiences often influence your current emotions, sense of self-worth, or patterns of undesirable behavior?

a) Yes

b) No

3. Do you feel pressured by societal standards and expectations?

a) Yes

b) No

4. Are you afraid to show your true self to others, fearing judgment or rejection?

   a) Yes

   b) No

Scoring

If you answered "Yes" to most questions, you may be facing significant barriers to inner love. Consider seeking support and using the techniques discussed in this chapter to address these barriers.

If you answered "No" to most questions, you may already be working through some barriers. However, continue to stay mindful of areas where you can grow to further enhance your self-awareness.

A. Reflect and Practice Self-Compassion

As you continue this practice, take time to reflect on your progress. Celebrate your successes and practice self-compassion. Remember, changing thought patterns takes time and effort.

Exercise: Weekly Reflection

1. **Review the Week:** At the end of each week, review your journal entries and reflections.

2. **Acknowledge Progress:** Write down any positive changes or insights you've noticed.
3. **Practice Self-Compassion:** Write a compassionate note to yourself, acknowledging your efforts and encouraging yourself to keep going.

Example Reflection

Date: July 1, 2099

Weekly Reflection: This week, I noticed that I'm becoming more aware of my negative thoughts. I successfully reframed "I can't do anything right" to "I made a mistake, but I can learn from it." I feel more hopeful and less critical of myself.

Self-Compassion Note: "I'm proud of myself for taking steps to change my thought patterns. It's okay to have setbacks, and I am doing my best. I am worthy of love and compassion."

Your Reflection

Date: _____

Weekly Reflection:

_____

_____

Self-Compassion Note:

_____

_____

Acknowledging the Journey

Recognizing and acknowledging these barriers is a crucial step in cultivating inner love. It's not about eliminating them overnight but about taking small, consistent steps to work through them. Remember, this journey is a marathon, not a sprint. Be patient and compassionate with yourself as you navigate these challenges.

By becoming aware of these barriers, challenging negative thoughts, addressing past traumas, redefining success, and embracing vulnerability, you can begin to break down the walls that stand between you and inner love. In Chapter 6, you will learn how to navigate and heal past wounds through techniques like writing a compassionate letter.

Ready to tackle the next steps? Let's dive deeper into the process of embracing vulnerability in the next chapter. It's going to be an enlightening and empowering ride!

CHAPTER 3

EMBRACING VULNERABILITY IN SELF-AWARENESS

Imagine attending a masquerade ball. Everyone wears convoluted masks, and while the masks are beautiful, they conceal the true faces of those behind them. Now, consider how many of us go through life behind a metaphorical mask hiding our true selves out of fear of judgment or rejection. This mask may protect us from the harsh glare of the outside world, but it also keeps us from fully discovering and expressing who we truly are. Embracing vulnerability is like taking off that mask, revealing our authentic selves, and allowing others to see us for who we truly are.

The Heart of Vulnerability
What if the very thing you've been avoiding is the key to everything you've been searching for? Vulnerability—it's a word that makes most of us uncomfortable. We've been conditioned to see it as a weakness, as exposure to risk. But what if we've been looking at it all wrong?

What if vulnerability isn't about exposing your wounds, but about embracing your strength? The strength to say, "This is me. All of me. The parts I love and the parts I'm still learning to love."

When you dare to be vulnerable, you give yourself permission to be seen—not as the polished, perfect version you think the world expects, but as the real, raw, beautifully imperfect human that you are. And here's something interesting: most people care less about how you look and more about how you act—your attitude, your energy, and the way you show up in the world. Recognizing this shifts your focus from external appearances to what truly matters—your internal dialogue, your thoughts, and the way you carry yourself from within.

And in that space, magic happens. You connect—truly connect—with others, with yourself, and with life in ways that are deep and meaningful. Vulnerability is where your true power lies. It's the birthplace of love, belonging, joy, and creativity.

So, take off the mask. Let the world see the real you. You might just discover that you are more powerful, more beautiful, and more courageous than you ever imagined.

Techniques for Embracing and Expressing Vulnerability

A. Start with Self-Compassion

Before you can be vulnerable with others, you must first be kind to yourself. Self-compassion means treating yourself with the same kindness and understanding that you would offer a dear friend. It's about acknowledging your imperfections and accepting them without harsh judgment. As you move through the pages of this book, you'll find thoughtfully curated exercises designed to help you recognize moments of self-criticism and transform them into self-compassion. For practical guidance, refer to the exercises in Chapter Five.

B. Practice Mindfulness

Mindfulness isn't about emptying your mind or escaping reality—it's about arriving fully in the present moment, just as you are. It's about sitting with yourself, embracing your thoughts, emotions, and sensations, and saying, "I am here. I am present. I am enough." Mindfulness is the practice of pausing, breathing, and allowing yourself to feel everything—without judgment, without the need to fix or change anything. Just being It's in these quiet moments that you learn to see yourself clearly, love yourself deeply, and accept yourself fully.

Imagine waking up each day with a sense of peace that isn't tied to external circumstances—a peace that comes from knowing that no matter what unfolds, you have the power to face it with grace and presence. This is the gift of mindfulness. It brings you back to yourself, to the truth of who you are beneath the noise and chaos of life. It reminds you that you are not your thoughts, your fears, your beliefs, or your past experiences—you are the awareness that holds it all with love and compassion. So, take a deep breath, let it fill your lungs, and remind yourself: In this very moment, I am exactly where I need to be.

Psychological research has shown that mindfulness enhances emotional awareness and regulation, allowing you to acknowledge and accept your vulnerabilities without judgment. By doing so, you embrace your authentic self and cultivate deeper connections with others. In Chapter Five, we will explore this further.

C. Share Your Story

Embracing vulnerability can be profoundly transformative, and one of the most powerful ways to do this is by sharing your story with others. As Arthur C. Brooks, a professor at Harvard University, and Oprah Winfrey discuss in their book Build the Life You Want: The Art and Science of Getting Happier, happiness is deeply tied to connection and sharing. In an interview, Brooks stated, "The key to happiness is sharing it." This means that opening up about your experiences—not necessarily to the entire world, but to trusted friends or loved ones—can be incredibly healing. It fosters deeper connections, mutual understanding, and a sense of belonging.

On the other hand, I firmly believe that there is a profound relationship between the ideal self and creative ideas. When we allow ourselves to be vulnerable, to share not only our struggles but also our aspirations, we open up pathways for innovation and deeper self-awareness. Creativity often emerges from a space of authenticity—when we are unafraid to express our truest thoughts, dreams, and experiences. By embracing vulnerability and sharing our personal journeys, we not only strengthen our relationships but also unlock creative potential, shaping a reality that aligns with our ideal selves.

D. Embrace Failure and Imperfection

We often avoid vulnerability because we fear failure of what others think of us and imperfection. However, accepting these aspects as natural parts of life allows us to grow and learn. Embrace your mistakes and imperfections as opportunities for growth rather than as evidence of inadequacy.

3.1 Stories of Transformation Through Vulnerability

Jane's Journey to Authenticity

Jane was always the one who seemed to have it all together. The perfect career, the flawless public image, the never-ending list of achievements—she was the quintessential overachiever, constantly striving to meet the high expectations she set for herself. But behind the polished exterior, Jane was crumbling under the weight of anxiety and self-doubt. Every day felt like a battle to keep up the façade of perfection, leaving her exhausted and disconnected from her true self.

"Why do I always feel like I'm not enough?" Jane would wonder late at night, staring at the ceiling as sleep evaded her. "No matter how much I accomplish, there's always this void. What am I missing?"

One day, after yet another sleepless night filled with racing thoughts, Jane made a bold decision. She reached out to a close friend and, for the first time, opened up about the struggles she had been hiding. Her voice trembled as she admitted her fears and insecurities. "I feel like I'm constantly wearing a mask," she confessed. "I'm scared that if I take it off, no one will like what they see." She added.

She braced herself for judgment or pity, fearing that her vulnerability would only expose her weaknesses. But instead, her friend responded with something Jane hadn't expected: empathy. Her friend didn't just listen; she shared her own struggles, revealing that behind her own polished exterior were similar feelings of doubt and anxiety.

"You're not alone in feeling this way," her friend said gently. "I often worry that I'm not good enough either."

In that moment of shared vulnerability, something profound shifted for Jane. The burden she had been carrying alone suddenly felt lighter. "So, it's not just me?" she thought, a mix of relief and disbelief washing over her. She realized that she wasn't alone in her struggles—that perfection wasn't a prerequisite for love or acceptance. The connection she felt in that honest exchange was deeper and more real than any achievement she had ever chased.

"Maybe I've been chasing the wrong kind of success," Jane reflected. "Maybe true fulfillment comes from being genuine, not perfect."

This moment was a turning point for Jane. She began to let go of the need to be perfect and allowed herself to be seen as she truly was, flaws and all. Embracing vulnerability became her path to authenticity, and as she opened up to others, she discovered that genuine connections were built not on perfection, but on honesty and empathy.

Jane's journey is a powerful reminder that we don't have to be perfect to be worthy of love and acceptance. If you're hiding behind a façade, afraid to show your true self, take a lesson from Jane: dare to be vulnerable. Share your struggles, your fears, and your imperfections. You might be surprised to find that what you see as flaws are the very things that will connect you more deeply with others.

Let go of the need to have it all together. Embrace your authentic self, and watch as your relationships evolve from surface-level interactions to deep, soul-nourishing connections. Remember, it's not perfection that makes us lovable—it's our willingness to be real. Take that step today. Open up, and experience the freedom and peace that come with living authentically—you may even discover a spark for growth and creativity along the way.

Martin's Fear of Rejection
Martin had spent years hiding behind a carefully crafted mask of happiness and success. Outwardly, he appeared to have it all together—a stable job, a friendly demeanor, and a smile that never wavered. But beneath the surface, Martin was battling a relentless

storm of depression that he kept hidden from everyone. The fear of being judged or rejected if people knew the truth kept him locked in his own silent struggle. Each day, the mask felt more suffocating, but Martin couldn't bring himself to let it slip. He was terrified that showing his true self would lead to rejection and isolation.

Then came a day that changed everything. During a group therapy session, Martin found himself at a breaking point. The weight of pretending had become unbearable, and for the first time, he felt a flicker of hope that maybe, just maybe, he didn't have to carry his burden alone. With a deep breath and a racing heart, Martin decided to share his story. As he spoke, his voice wavered, but he kept going—admitting his struggles with depression, the mask he wore, and the fear that had kept him silent for so long.

The room fell silent as Martin finished speaking, and for a moment, he braced himself for the judgment he had always feared. But instead of rejection, he was met with something entirely different—overwhelming support and understanding. His peers didn't see him as weak or flawed; they saw him as courageous, human, and real. One by one, they opened up, sharing their own experiences, forming a circle of empathy and connection that Martin had never known. His vulnerability created a ripple effect, giving others the courage to share freely, unburdened by the fear of judgment.

That moment was transformative for Martin. He realized that the vulnerability he had feared for so long was not a weakness, but a powerful strength. By opening up, he hadn't pushed people away; he had drawn them closer. The walls he had built around himself began to crumble, replaced by genuine connections that felt like a lifeline. For the first time, Martin felt truly seen and accepted—not for the mask he wore, but for who he really was.

Martin's journey is a powerful reminder that vulnerability is not something to be feared—it is a bridge to deeper connection and personal growth. If you've been hiding behind a facade, afraid to show your true self, take a step toward openness. Share your story, your struggles, and your fears. You may find that what you once believed would drive people away is actually what brings them closer.

When we allow ourselves to share freely, we often create a deeper sense of support and understanding, dissolving the illusion of rejection and judgment. Let Martin's story inspire you to embrace your own vulnerability. It is in those moments of raw honesty that we discover the strength to connect, to heal, and to grow.

Don't let the fear of rejection keep you from the connections that could change your life. Take off the mask, let yourself be seen, and experience the profound power of authenticity. As we've seen before, the very things you fear are often the very things that set you free.

Claire's Artistic Expression

Claire was a gifted artist, but her talent was hidden away in sketchbooks and canvases that rarely saw the light of day. Each piece she created was a window into her soul, capturing her deepest thoughts and emotions. But Claire's fear of criticism kept her from sharing her art with the world. The idea of exposing her innermost self to the judgment of others was terrifying. She convinced herself that her work wasn't good enough, that it was safer to keep it all tucked away where no one could see.

But the longing to be seen and understood never left her. One day, with her heart pounding and self-doubt swirling, Claire decided to take a leap of faith. She mustered the courage to display her artwork at a local gallery, despite the voice in her head telling her to turn back. As she set up her pieces, each one felt like an act of vulnerability, a silent confession of her fears, hopes, and dreams.

The night of the gallery opening, Claire braced herself for the worst, expecting criticism or, even worse, indifference. But as the evening unfolded, something extraordinary happened. People were drawn to her art, not just admiring its beauty, but connecting deeply with the stories it told. Strangers shared how her paintings resonated with their own experiences, how they saw pieces of themselves in her work. The feedback was overwhelmingly positive, but more than that, it was affirming. Claire's art had touched people's lives in ways she had never imagined.

This moment was a revelation for Claire. She realized that her art, born from her most vulnerable places, had the power to reach others on a profound level. By opening up and sharing her creativity, she wasn't just displaying paintings; she was offering pieces of herself, inviting others to connect, to feel, and to reflect. The very act of being vulnerable, which she had once feared, became her greatest strength.

Claire's confidence soared as she continued to share her art with the world. She embraced her identity as an artist, no longer hiding in the shadows of self-doubt. Each piece she created and shared was a reminder that true impact comes from authenticity and the courage to be seen. Claire discovered that vulnerability wasn't a weakness—it was a bridge that connected her to others, allowing her to make a meaningful impact through her creativity.

Claire's journey is a powerful reminder that the world needs your unique voice, your story, and your creativity. If you've been holding back, afraid to share your gifts with the world, take a lesson from Claire: dare to be vulnerable. Show up as you are, with all your imperfections, and let your light shine. You never know whose life you might touch when you choose to be authentically you.

Let go of the fear of criticism and embrace the courage to be seen. Your creativity has the power to inspire, to heal, and to connect. Take that leap, share your gifts, and watch as the world opens up in response to your bravery.

The Empowering Journey of Vulnerability

Embracing vulnerability is a courageous and transformative journey. It requires peeling away the masks we wear, acknowledging our limitations, and allowing ourselves to form genuine connections. The challenge lies in recognizing that within our minds, two images coexist: the perceived self—the version of ourselves shaped by our conscious thoughts and experiences—and the ideal self—the version we aspire to be, deeply embedded within our subconscious mind.

Understanding this duality is key to self-awareness. When we bridge the gap between who we believe we are and who we truly desire to become, vulnerability shifts from being a source of fear to a powerful tool for growth, authenticity, and deeper connection with ourselves and others. By practicing self-compassion, mindfulness, and sharing our stories, we cultivate a deeper sense of inner love and authenticity—both of which are essential in revealing our ideal self.

Through this process, we not only embrace our true essence but also create the space for genuine transformation, where vulnerability becomes the bridge between who we are and who we are meant to be.

> *"The very best and highest attainment in this life is to remain still and let God act and speak in you." – Meister Eckhart*

As you embark on this journey, remember that vulnerability is not a sign of weakness but a powerful strength. It allows you to connect with your true self and with others, fostering meaningful relationships and personal growth. Embrace your vulnerability, celebrate your imperfections, and let your authentic self-shine.

Ready to dive deeper into practical steps for cultivating inner love? Let's continue this journey together in the next chapter. It's time to explore the daily practices and rituals that can help you nurture and sustain your inner love. Let's go!

Why Vulnerability is Essential

"What lies behind us and what lies before us are tiny matters compared to what lies within us." – Ralph Waldo Emerson

Vulnerability is the cornerstone of authentic living and personal growth. It involves exposing your true self—your fears, dreams, and flaws—despite the risk of judgment or rejection. When you embrace vulnerability, you open the door to deeper connections, genuine relationships, and a more fulfilling life.

Psychologically, vulnerability helps you have increased empathy, compassion, and resilience. By embracing vulnerability, you can break down barriers and create more meaningful and sincere relationships.

Real-Life Examples
Overcoming Fear of Judgment
Carol was known for her impeccable image—the polished demeanor, the flawless resume, and the unwavering smile. But behind the carefully curated facade, she carried an exhausting weight. No one saw the anxiety she battled daily or the relentless voice inside her head insisting she maintain perfection at all costs. Perfection was her shield, but it had also become her prison.

For years, she avoided anything that might expose her flaws. At work, she took on projects that reinforced her reputation as competent and reliable, even if it meant sacrificing sleep. In social settings, she carefully filtered what she shared, afraid that any sign of vulnerability might shatter the image she had worked so hard to maintain. On the outside, her life appeared perfect; on the inside, it felt hollow.

Then came a particularly exhausting week. At a work event, Carol found herself surrounded by colleagues who seemed to navigate networking with ease. Beneath her composed exterior, self-doubt simmered. But then, she overheard a colleague she deeply admired admit—casually yet sincerely—how stress had been affecting her work. It was a simple moment of honesty, but it hit Carol like a revelation. Here was someone she viewed as successful and composed, openly acknowledging a struggle she, too, understood.

This reminded me of my younger years when I hesitated to contribute to casual conversations, held back by thoughts like, What if I speak and what I say doesn't make sense? or What if my words don't matter at all? I remained silent, fearing I would look foolish. But when I finally opened up and found strength in sharing my story, everything shifted. I started speaking freely, with confidence, realizing that my voice mattered. Even when my words didn't immediately resonate, I learned to recognize patterns, refine my thoughts, and grow from the experience.

Inspired by this unexpected honesty, Carol made a decision. She didn't have to take the leap all at once, but she could start small. The next time she met with her close friend, instead of glossing over her struggles, she shared a little bit of her truth—how she felt overwhelmed, how she often wondered if she was good enough. She didn't need to perform or impress; she just needed to be real.

> *"Our doubts are traitors and make us lose the good we often might win, by fearing to attempt." – William Shakespeare*

Her friend's reaction was not one of judgment, but of relief and recognition. "I feel the same way sometimes," her friend said. And just like that, the walls Carol had built around herself began to crumble. It wasn't a grand gesture, but it was a crack in the armor that allowed for something real to seep in.

Carol began to realize that the pressure she felt was largely self-imposed. She didn't need to be perfect to be valued. In fact, it was her willingness to be open—if only a little—that made her feel truly connected. She started approaching her relationships differently, allowing herself to show up as she was, without the need to perform or maintain an image that wasn't truly her.

Carol's story is a testament to the idea that change often begins with a small step—a conversation, an honest moment, a shared struggle. If you've been hiding behind the need to be perfect, consider letting your guard down, even just a little. You don't have to dismantle your defenses all at once; simply start by being a bit more honest, a bit more real.

I've personally witnessed how much deeper my connections feel when I share my story without expectations or fear of judgment. Yes, criticism sometimes follows, and at times, I feel the sting of vulnerability. But through reflection, I've learned to transform those criticisms into motivation for growth rather than allowing them to silence me. Napoleon Hill, in The Law of Success, put it best: "The easiest way to avoid criticism is to be nothing and do nothing—the remedy never fails."

If you live in fear of judgment, you may also rob yourself of the chance to connect, grow, and truly experience life. Your worth isn't defined by perfection, but by your courage to show up as you are.

3.2 Practical Exercises

The Courageous Conversation and Self-Compassion Journal

A. **1. The Courageous Conversation**

This is an interactive exercise designed to help you embrace vulnerability, express your truth, and overcome the fear of judgment. It encourages open and honest dialogue—whether with yourself or others—by confronting difficult emotions, sharing personal experiences, and fostering deeper connections.

Note: Keep this interactive experience as a reminder of your courage and commitment to personal growth.

Step 1: Identifying Someone You Trust

Think about someone in your life whom you trust deeply. This person should be someone who has shown understanding, support, and empathy towards you.

Name of the person: _____

Why do you trust this person?
Write a few sentences explaining why you feel comfortable sharing with this person.

_____

_____

_____

Step 2: Planning the Conversation

Choose a time and place where you both can have an uninterrupted conversation. It could be over a cup of coffee, a walk in the park, or a quiet evening at home.

Preferred time and place: _____

Why did you choose this setting?

Write a few sentences about why this setting is conducive for an open conversation.

_____

_____

_____

Step 3: Deciding What to Share

Reflect on what part of your story you want to share. This could be a fear you've been holding onto, a past mistake that haunts you, or a dream that you've been too afraid to pursue.

What do you want to share?

Write down what you plan to share.

_____

_____

Why is this important to you?

Reflect on why sharing this is significant for your personal growth and the relationship.

_____
_____
_____
_____

Step 4: Preparing Yourself

Take a moment to breathe and gather your thoughts. Remember, the goal is to be open and honest, and to notice how this affects both your relationship and your sense of self.

How do you feel about sharing this part of your story?
Write down your current feelings.

_____
_____
_____

What are your hopes for this conversation?
Write down what you hope to achieve or understand through this conversation.

_____
_____
_____

Step 5: Having the Conversation

When the time comes, approach the conversation with an open heart and mind. This not only helps you regulate your emotions but also heightens your awareness of your surroundings. Speak honestly, listen attentively, and remain present in the moment. Pay attention to how this openness influences your relationship and deepens your sense of self.

Date and time of the conversation: _____

Location: _____

Step 6: Reflecting on the Experience

After the conversation, take some time to reflect on how it went

How did the conversation go?

Write a few sentences about how the conversation unfolded.

_____
_____
_____

How did sharing make you feel?

Reflect on your emotions after sharing your story.

_____
_____
_____

How did this affect your relationship?

Write down any changes you noticed in your relationship.

_____
_____
_____

What did you learn about yourself?

Take a moment to reflect on any new insights or realizations you've gained. If you prepared well, you may notice recurring patterns that surfaced during your conversation—patterns that likely mirrored the thoughts and emotions you experienced while preparing for the meeting. This is the power of self-awareness. It reveals how your internal world shapes your external experiences, reinforcing the understanding that your life unfolds as a series of predetermined events within your own awareness.

_____
_____
_____

Reflect on what you are grateful for after attending the meeting.

_____
_____
_____

Follow-up Plan

Based on your experience, what steps will you take next? Write down any actions or follow-ups you plan to take.

_____
_____
_____

Step 7: Continuing the Journey

Remember, this is a part of your ongoing journey of self-discovery and inner love. Celebrate the courage it took to share your story and use this experience to continue growing and nurturing your inner love.

A note to yourself: Write a few sentences of encouragement and acknowledgment to yourself for taking this courageous step.

_____
_____
_____

B. The Self-Compassion Journal

Self-compassion involves treating yourself with the same kindness and understanding that you would offer a friend. This exercise will guide you through identifying moments of self-criticism and transform them with compassion.

Step 1: Setting Up Your Journal

Choose a journal or a digital document where you can regularly write down your thoughts. This will be your safe space for self-reflection and self-compassion.

Journal Name: _____

Start Date: _____

Step 2: Identifying Moments of Self-Criticism

Think about recent moments when you were critical of yourself. These could be related to work, relationships, personal goals, or everyday tasks.

1ST Moment of Self-Criticism

Describe the situation where you were critical of yourself

_____
_____
_____

2ND Moment of Self-Criticism

Describe another situation where you were critical of yourself

3ᴿᴰ Moment of Self-Criticism

Describe a third situation where you were critical of yourself

Step 3: Transforming with Compassion

For each moment of self-criticism, write down a more compassionate response. Imagine you are speaking to a dear friend who is going through the same situation.

1ˢᵀ Transforming Moment of Self-Criticism

Self-Criticism

Compassionate Response

2ᴺᴰ Transforming Moment of Self-Criticism

Self-Criticism

_____
_____
_____

Compassionate Response

_____
_____
_____

3RD Transforming Moment of Self-Criticism #3

Self-Criticism

_____
_____
_____

Compassionate Response

_____
_____

Step 4: Reflecting on the Process

Take some time to reflect on how reframing your self-criticism with compassion made you feel.

How did reframing these moments make you feel?

Write down your reflections

_____
_____

What insights did you gain about yourself?

Reflect on any new understandings or insights you gained through this process.

_____

_____

_____

Step 5: Regular Practice

Commit to making this a regular practice. Set aside time each day or week to write in your self-compassion journal.

Frequency of Writing: _____

Reminder Time: _____

Note to Self

Write a note of encouragement to remind yourself why this practice is important:

_____

_____

_____

Step 6: Celebrating Progress

Periodically review your journal entries to see how far you've come. Celebrate your progress and acknowledge the effort you've put into being kind to yourself.

Review Date: _____

Reflections on Progress

Write down your thoughts on your progress
_____
_____
_____

Step 1: Final Affirmation

Write an affirmation to reinforce your commitment to self-compassion
_____
_____

Note: Keep this interactive experience as a testament to your journey towards greater self-compassion and inner love.

C. Guided meditation

Full Body Relaxation and Awareness

Welcome to this guided meditation. This practice will guide you through a full-body relaxation exercise to help you release tension, calm your mind, and foster a deep connection with yourself. Let's begin.

Find a quiet, comfortable place where you can sit or lie down without distractions. Close your eyes if you feel comfortable, and inhale through your nose, hold it for a moment, and exhale slowly through your mouth. Allow your body to settle and relax.
Bring your attention to your toes. Imagine a warm, soothing light gently touching them. With each inhale, feel this light filling your toes with relaxation, and with each exhale, release any tension.

Let this warm light slowly spread to the soles of your feet. Notice the sensations—perhaps a gentle tingling or a feeling of softness as you allow the light to relax your feet completely.
Move your awareness Up the Body

Guide the light towards your ankles and calves. Feel it soothing these areas, melting away any tightness or discomfort. Breathe deeply, welcome the sense of ease.

Guide the light up to your knees and thighs. With each inhale, feel them growing heavy, relaxed, and grounded and with each exhale release all tension.
 Bring your awareness to your hips and lower back. Imagine the warm light enveloping this area as you inhale, easing any tension as you exhale.

Bring the light to your stomach and chest. Notice how each inhale feels here—natural, effortless and exhale releasing any tension in this area. Feel your chest rise as you inhale and fall as you exhale, fill a sense of peace as the light spreads throughout this area.

Bring your focus to your shoulders and arms feeling a soothing light as you inhale and the release of tightness as you exhale.

Gently direct the light to your neck and jaw. Soften these areas as you inhale, dissolving any tightness as you exhale.
Finally, guide the warm light to your face and head. Feel your forehead soften, your eyes relax as you inhale, and your scalp release any residual tension as you exhale.

Take a moment to notice the calmness and relaxation throughout your body. Feel the stillness, that sense of peace. Stay here for as long as you need, simply observing your breath and the ease you've cultivated.

When you're ready, gently bring your awareness back to the present moment. Wiggle your fingers and toes, stretch lightly, and open your eyes.

How are you feeling?

☐ Calm ☐ Connected ☐ Relaxed. ☐ Centered
☐ Anxious _____

If you're feeling any negative emotions, that's completely okay. Acknowledge these feelings with kindness and gratitude for taking the time to care for yourself. The fact that you showed up for this practice is a meaningful step forward. Remember, you can always return to this meditation whenever you need to, giving yourself another chance to cultivate calm and balance. Take it one step at a time—each effort makes a difference.

As you continue this journey of self-awareness, you will be introduced to a variety of meditations tailored to specific activities and intentions. Each practice will guide you deeper into mindfulness, self-compassion, and emotional balance, helping you align your mind, body, and spirit with your unique needs. Whether you seek relaxation, focus, or emotional healing, these meditations will become valuable tools on your path to inner peace and personal growth.

D. The Failure Celebration

Step 1: Identifying a Recent Failure or Mistake

Think about a recent failure or mistake you experienced. It could be something at work, in your personal life, or a goal you didn't achieve.

Describe the Failure or Mistake

What happened?

_____

_____

Why do you consider this a failure or mistake?

_____

_____

Step 2: Reflecting on the Experience

Take some time to reflect on what you learned from this experience. Every failure has valuable lessons that contribute to personal growth.

What did you learn from this experience?

Write down the lessons you learned

_____

_____

How has this failure or mistake helped you grow?
Reflect on the ways this experience has contributed to your personal development.

_____

_____

Step 3: Celebrating the Lessons Learned
Celebrating your growth and resilience is an important part of turning failures into positive experiences. Choose a small act of kindness to treat yourself and acknowledge your efforts.

How will you celebrate your lessons learned?

Choose an act of kindness toward yourself (e.g., treating yourself to your favorite meal, taking a relaxing walk, spending time with a loved one)

_____

_____

When will you do this?
Set a specific date and time for your celebration

_____

Step 4: Reflecting on Your Celebration

After you have celebrated your growth, take a moment to reflect on how it made you feel and what you gained from this process.

How did the celebration make you feel?
Write down your feelings after celebrating the lessons you've learned

_____
_____

What did you gain from this experience?
Reflect on the impact of celebrating your growth and how it has reinforced your resilience

_____
_____

Step 5: Continuing the Practice

Make a commitment to regularly celebrate your growth and resilience by turning failures into positive experiences.

How often will you practice this?

Decide on a frequency for reflecting on and celebrating your failures (e.g., monthly, quarterly)

___

Reminder

Set a reminder to regularly practice the failure celebration exercise

___

Note to Self

Write a note of encouragement to remind yourself why it's important to celebrate your growth.

___
___
___
___
___
___
___
___

Final Affirmation

Write an affirmation to reinforce your commitment to celebrating your growth

_____
_____
_____
_____
_____
_____
_____
_____
_____

Keep this interactive experience as a reminder of your ability to turn failures into valuable lessons and opportunities for self-kindness and growth.

CHAPTER 4

PRACTICAL STEPS TO CULTIVATE INNER LOVE

Magic of Loving Yourself

There's always that one driver who can turn a peaceful commute into chaos. Picture this: I'm behind the wheel of my friend's futuristic Bentley, completely immersed in its beauty. The sleek curves, luxurious interior, and the smooth purr of the engine made it feel like I was gliding on a cloud. Everything was perfect—until he showed up. Mr. Speedy, who decided rush hour was the perfect time to audition his inner "Fast and Furious." He zipped dangerously close to the car ahead of me, forcing me to hit the brakes as though he had sliced right through my lane. The Bentley, ever responsive and poised, handled it effortlessly. Still, it was clear Mr. Speedy had no idea what kind of car he was messing with.

The truth was, my Bentley could have left him in the dust without breaking a sweat. For a fleeting moment, I felt the urge to prove it. I could see him through his rear window, fidgeting in his seat and stealing glances at me in his rearview mirror, clearly showing off and hoping to provoke a race. My heart raced, and adrenaline surged. For just a second, I imagined pressing the pedal and showing Mr. Speedy who the real boss was. But then, something caught my attention. I glanced up at a digital billboard, and the words popped up in big, bold letters: "All you need is Love," in green, blue, white, and red. It was as if the universe had stepped in to calm my racing heart and remind me of what truly mattered. I took a deep breath, let the message sink in, and smiled. Mr. Speedy could have his moment; I had something far more precious peace of mind, a beautiful Bentley, and the reminder that love is all you need, even on the wildest commutes.

In that instant, I realized that love isn't just a lofty ideal—it's a choice we make in every moment, even in the most stressful situations. And it starts with the love we give ourselves. By choosing love over ego, I kept my peace intact and stayed true to who I am. This moment was a powerful reminder that in a world full of chaos, the greatest power we have is the love we cultivate within ourselves.

So, the next time life throws a challenge your way, remember that the real victory isn't in winning the race, but in how you choose to respond. As Stephen R. Covey explains in his book, The 7 Habits of Highly Effective People, "Between stimulus and response, there is a space. In that space lies our freedom and power to choose our response. In our response lies our growth and our happiness."

Let your response in that space be rooted in love—love for yourself, for others, and for the journey you're on. By anchoring your choices in love, you not only navigate challenges with grace but also create harmony and fulfillment in your life. Let inner love guide your responses, and you'll discover that no matter how wild the ride, you can always stay in control.

Daily Habits for Sustaining Inner love

"The journey of a thousand miles begins with one step." – Lao Tzu

Maintaining inner love requires consistent nurturing through daily habits. Nearly 99% of our actions are habitual, carried out automatically without conscious choice—even our bad habits are rooted in a particular state of consciousness. By intentionally shaping your daily routines, you can reinforce a mindset of inner-love and emotional well-being. Here are some powerful habits to help sustain you inner Love journey.

A. Daily Affirmations: Speak Life into your soul

Think of affirmations as seeds planted in the garden of your mind. At first, they may feel foreign, like words you don't quite believe, and resistance will rise within you. This is the natural discomfort of replacing old habits with new ones—the pull of the comfort zone holding on. As the saying goes, old habits die hard. You might find inspiration in James Clear's Atomic Habits, where he suggests linking new habits with existing ones to ease the transition. Through consistent effort and discipline, affirmations will begin to take root, and what once felt unnatural will soon flow effortlessly. Over time, you will feel a shift—inner love, peace, and self-acceptance will no longer be fleeting moments but a natural state of being.

Just as a seed needs water, sunlight, and time to grow, the words you speak to yourself require repetition, belief, and aligned action to take hold. It's not merely about repeating words in the mirror—it's about speaking life into your soul. It's about looking into your own eyes, beyond the layers of doubt and fear, and declaring with certainty, "I am enough." "I am worthy of love." "I am capable of growth and change." You are not simply speaking empty words; it is the energy and feeling behind them that matter. Every word carries a frequency, a vibration that echoes through your subconscious, influencing your perception of reality. Just as sound waves ripple through the air, the energy behind your words imprints itself on your inner dialogue, thus influencing how you see yourself and the world. Affirmations are like programming code for the mind. Just as a computer executes the commands it receives; your subconscious mind carries out the beliefs you reinforce through repetition and feeling. Whether rooted in faith, quantum energy, or brain rewiring, the mechanism is the same: what you consistently affirm or do is what shapes your reality.

As the Bible states in John 1:1, "In the beginning was the Word, and the Word was with God, and the Word was God." Neville Goddard builds on this, explaining that "The Word is the inner dialogue that runs ceaselessly in your mind." If that dialogue is filled with thoughts of lack, then lack will shape your experience. If it is filled with abundance, success, and love, then that is what will materialize in your life.

This is why affirmations should be spoken as if they are already true. Your subconscious mind does not distinguish between what is real and what is assumed—it simply accepts whatever is impressed upon it. When you affirm, I am or I have, you are not waiting for a future reality; you are claiming it in the present. Your consciousness exists in the eternal now, and what you repeatedly focus on becomes the foundation upon which your life is built.

Begin each day with a moment of stillness. Close your eyes, take a deep breath, and allow your affirmations to flow through you with intention. Feel the weight of your words sink into your being, like gentle waves reshaping the shore. Let them wash away the doubts, the old conditioning, and the stories that no longer serve you. In time, these words will no longer feel separate from you—they will become you. You will hear them reflected in your inner voice, woven into the fabric of your thoughts, shifting the way you see yourself and the world. And when this happens, something powerful awakens within you—the energy to create, to act, and to manifest the reality you have been affirming all along.

Your brain is a masterpiece of adaptability, capable of rewiring itself through a process known as neuroplasticity. With every repetition of a positive affirmation, you are strengthening neural pathways associated with self-worth, confidence, and gratitude. Scientific research confirms that affirmations activate regions of the brain tied to positive self-perception, reinforcing emotional resilience and shifting the way you respond to life. Remember, it is not the words alone that hold power—it is the feeling and belief behind them, the unwavering conviction that fuels them. Speak with authority, believe with certainty, and watch as your reality transforms to match the truth you have claimed.

Exercise: The Morning Affirmation Routine

Each morning, stand in front of the mirror, look yourself in the eye, and speak three affirmations that resonate with your deepest desires. Choose words that align with what you need to hear most, allowing them to connect with your heart and reinforce the reality you wish to create. For example, say:

"I am worthy of love and respect."

"I am capable of achieving my goals."

"I am enough, just as I am."

Note: Repeat these affirmations with conviction and notice how they set a positive tone for your day.

B. Meditation: Finding Peace Within

Meditation is a transformative practice that fosters self-awareness, inner peace, and mindful presence. By directing focused attention—whether through breath control, visualization, or mantra repetition—you train the mind to cultivate a state of calm and clarity. Through regular practice, meditation allows individuals to move beyond habitual thought patterns and experience greater mental and emotional freedom.

A key physiological benefit of meditation is its engagement of the parasympathetic nervous system, which promotes relaxation and healing. This shift moves the body away from the stress-induced "fight-or-flight" response, governed by the sympathetic nervous system, and into a calm, restorative state essential for overall well-being. By consistently practicing meditation, individuals can rewire their brains for resilience, emotional balance, and greater well-being

As Dr. Joe Dispenza explains in his book Becoming Supernatural, meditation is a transformative practice that impacts both mental and physical health. He emphasizes that consistent meditation not only reduces stress and anxiety but also harnesses the brain's ability to rewire itself through neuroplasticity—the brain's capacity to create new neural connections and change its structure over time. When we meditate, we "disconnect from the outer world" and allow the brain to rest and reorganize itself, which facilitates the formation of new neural pathways that support healthier thought patterns and emotional responses (Dispenza, 2017).

Dr. Dispenza further highlights the importance of activating the parasympathetic nervous system through meditation. He notes that this process can lower cortisol levels, improve heart rate variability (HRV), and foster a deeper connection between the mind and body.

By regularly entering a relaxed, heart-centered state, we can "train our body to operate from a place of coherence rather than chaos" (Dispenza, 2017). This coherence is essential for cultivating inner love, as it aligns our emotional and physical states, leading to a more harmonious and balanced life.

Meditation has been scientifically shown to activate the parasympathetic nervous system, leading to reduced cortisol levels and improved heart rate variability, which are crucial for promoting relaxation. Research indicates that regular meditation practice can lead to significant changes in brain structure and function through neuroplasticity, enabling the formation of new neural pathways that enhance emotional regulation and reduce stress and anxiety. For example, a study published in *Psychiatry Research: Neuroimaging* found that participants who practiced mindfulness meditation exhibited increased gray matter density in brain regions associated with self-awareness and emotional regulation, demonstrating that meditation not only calms the mind but also rewires it for healthier thought patterns and emotional responses. This transformative practice fosters a deep connection between mind and body, facilitating a journey toward inner peace and emotional freedom.

By engaging in regular meditation, we invite healing, growth, and a deeper connection to ourselves. This practice becomes not merely a tool for stress management, but a gateway to transformation. In cultivating this connection between mind and body, as Dr. Dispenza describes, we open ourselves to experience greater emotional freedom and inner peace—a journey back to love and wholeness.

Integrating Meditation into Your Journey of Inner Love

Drawing from Dr. Dispenza's insights, meditation emerges as a powerful tool for nurturing inner love. It is more than just calming the mind; it is a holistic practice that creates the ideal conditions for the body to heal, the heart to open, and the spirit to expand. By incorporating meditation into your daily routine, you can deepen self-awareness and cultivate an inner harmony that naturally radiates outward, influencing your interactions and experiences.

As you continue through this book, you will find more exercises designed to guide you back to your own awareness. These practices will help you embrace each moment with a calm, open heart, allowing you to live more fully aligned with your true self and the love that resides within.

Simple Meditation Practice (10-15 minutes daily)

As discussed in the previous chapter, you were introduced to a comprehensive guided meditation. You can revisit that practice or simply follow the steps below for a daily mindfulness routine.

1. Choose a peaceful and comfortable place where you won't be disturbed.
2. Sit Comfortably on a chair, cushion, or floor, ensure that your posture is relaxed yet upright.
3. Gently close your eyes to minimize distractions and bring your focus inward.
   a. Inhale deeply through your nose for a count of four.
   b. Hold your breath for a count of four.
   c. Exhale slowly through your mouth for a count of four.
   d. Repeat this cycle, maintaining a steady and relaxed rhythm for 10 – 15 minutes
5. If your mind starts to wander or emotions arise, observe them without judgment. Gently redirect your awareness back to your breath.
6. With each inhale, imagine drawing in positive energy or recite positive affirmation for relaxation and with each exhale, visualize releasing tension and stress.

7. After 10-15 minutes, gently open your eyes and take a moment to appreciate the calmness you have cultivated.

To enhance Your Meditation Experience, consider using guided meditation tools such as: Calm, Headspace, or Tripp App (especially immersive within the Meta Quest 3 VR system)

Personally, I use Tripp App in the Meta Quest 3 VR system. This app creates an immersive experience, allowing me to momentarily escape the chaos of the world and enter a dedicated space for well-being and mindfulness.

By integrating meditation into your daily routine, you cultivate a deeper sense of calm, self-acceptance, and emotional balance.

C. Developing a Self-Care Routine

Self-care is not a luxury—it's a necessity. It's about dedicating time to nurture your physical, emotional, and mental well-being. Establishing a self-care routine is essential for maintaining a healthy relationship with yourself. As the saying goes, "Vitality is the course of life." This principle aligns with the law of consciousness, which operates vibrationally within your mind. When you cultivate self-care, you initiate a ripple effect—

enhancing your sense of balance, calmness, and emotional well-being. This, in turn, strengthens the law of attraction, drawing mutual respect, increased productivity, and deeper love into your life. By prioritizing self-care, you create a foundation that supports both your inner harmony and your external success.

Step-by-Step Guide to Creating a Self-Care Routine

1. Identify Your Needs

Start by identifying areas in your life where you need more care. This could be physical (like needing more sleep), emotional (like needing more time to unwind), or mental (like needing more time for hobbies).

2. Set Aside Time

Schedule dedicated time each day for self-care and treat it as non-negotiable—just like a meeting or a doctor's appointment. As Jim Rohn once said, "Work harder on yourself than you do on your job." Prioritizing self-care isn't selfish; it enhances your energy, productivity, and overall well-being, allowing you to show up as your best self in every area of life.

3. Choose Activities That Nourish You

Select activities that bring you joy and relaxation. This could be anything from taking a bubble bath, reading a positive book, practicing yoga, or going for a walk in nature.

4. Be Consistent

Consistency is the foundation of progress. Make self-care a regular part of your routine, not just a remedy for burnout. As mentioned earlier, consistency builds discipline, and discipline shapes habits—forming the bridge to resilience. When self-care becomes second nature, it strengthens your ability to navigate challenges, whether in relationships, business, or personal growth, allowing you to bounce back with greater ease and confidence.

Make Inner love a Habit

> *"We are what we repeatedly do. Excellence, then, is not an act, but a habit." – Aristotle*

Integrating inner love into your daily life eventually becomes a habit. Here are five practical tips to help you weave inner love into the fabric of your everyday existence:

1. Practice Mindful Eating

Pay attention to what you eat and how it makes you feel. Choose nourishing foods that energize and satisfy you. Take the time to savor each bite and appreciate the act of nourishing your body.

2. Set Healthy Boundaries

Learn to say no to activities and people that drain your energy. Prioritize your time and emotional well-being by setting clear boundaries that honor your needs. As you progress, you'll explore how to audit your relationships and prioritize connections that support your growth and well-being.

3. Engage in Physical Activity

Regular exercise is a powerful way to care for your body, build resilience, and ultimately cultivate self-love. Find an activity you enjoy—whether it's dancing, hiking, swimming, or yoga. Movement not only strengthens your body but also releases endorphins, boosting your mood, energy, and overall well-being.

4. Surround Yourself with Positivity

Surround yourself with people who uplift and support you. Engage in activities that bring you joy and fulfillment. Limit exposure to negative influences, whether it's toxic relationships or negative media.

5. Celebrate Your Achievements

Take time to acknowledge and celebrate your accomplishments, no matter how small. Recognizing your progress not only boosts self-esteem but also reinforces your sense of self-worth, motivating you to continue growing and thriving.

Integrating Inner love into Everyday Life

Mike was always on the move, his life a blur of emails, meetings, and a never-ending to-do list. To anyone looking in from the outside, he seemed like the poster child for productivity. But beneath the hustle and bustle, Mike felt like a ghost in his own life—present but not really living. His days were a series of motions on repeat, and he was beginning to feel the weight of it all pressing down on him like a heavy fog that just wouldn't lift.

One evening, after yet another day that had drained him to his core, Mike found himself standing in his kitchen, staring blankly out the window into the dark night. His own reflection stared back at him, and for a moment, he didn't recognize the tired, worn-out face in the glass. A tightness gripped his chest, and a thought struck him with a jolt: "I'm losing myself in all this noise." Then, almost like a whisper from deep within, another voice followed, softer yet clear: "You deserve better." It echoed with a memory from his younger days: "Remember how you used to run, feeling free and alive?" That thought was like a spark in the darkness, and in that moment, Mike knew something had to change. "If I could pour so much of me into work and everyone around me, why couldn't I invest a little of this energy back into me?" he thought.

Determined to turn things around, Mike started small. He knew that inner love didn't have to mean a complete life overhaul; it could begin with a few simple changes. So, he started with mindful eating. Instead of scarfing down a sandwich while answering emails, he made a conscious choice to prepare simple, healthy meals and sit down to enjoy them. At first, it felt forced, like he was playing a role in a movie. But as he practiced slowing down and actually tasting his food, he began to find moments of calm and peace amidst his chaotic days. His meals became his quiet rebellion against the autopilot that had been running his life, a small but profound way to reconnect with himself.

Feeling encouraged, Mike took a bolder step—setting boundaries at work. This was a big one. For years, he had been the "yes" guy—always available, always ready to jump in—but it had come at the cost of his own peace. The thought of saying "no" felt terrifying, even though sometimes it was the only answer that made sense. He soon realized that every "no" to someone else was really a "yes" to himself. By protecting his evenings and treating them as sacred time to recharge, he discovered it wasn't about shutting people out; it was about inviting himself in. To his surprise, the sky didn't fall, the world didn't end. Everything simply became a little quieter, a little calmer.

As Mike continued nurturing his inner love, a familiar echo surfaced in his mind: "Remember how you used to run, feeling free and alive?" This thought resonated with the positive changes he was experiencing, urging him to reconnect with that sense of freedom. Inspired, Mike laced up his sneakers and took to jogging. Initially, it was just an attempt to shake off the tension from sitting at a desk all day. However, with each stride, he began to feel a shift within. The rhythm of his feet hitting the pavement became a steady beat that synchronized with his breath, his thoughts, his heartbeat. Running transformed into a moving meditation—a way to clear his mind and feel his body come alive again. morning jog became a ritual of release—a chance to let go of yesterday's worries and start fresh.

I can relate to Mike's experience. For me, running or working out has become more than just breaking a sweat; it's where my mind finds its flow. Often, in the middle of a run, my thoughts drift into creative territory—ideas for my projects, like this very book, start to take shape. The physical act of running seems to unlock something in my mind, bringing clarity to a narrative I've been stuck on or revealing a new angle I hadn't considered. These runs have become the foundation of my creative process. Whenever I'm tempted to skip a workout, I remind myself that it's not just about staying fit; it's where I tap into my creativity and recharge my spirit.

Just like Mike, I've learned that small acts of inner love can ripple out into every aspect of life. As Mike continued to create these moments for himself, he noticed how his relationships began to change. He gravitated toward friends who lifted him up, who valued him for who he was—not just for what he could do. He began to celebrate his small victories, whether it was completing a project or simply making it through a tough day. Each celebration, no matter how small, became a powerful reminder that his worth wasn't tied only to productivity but also to the simple act of practicing inner love and kindness toward himself.

Mike's journey shows us that inner love doesn't require an earth-shattering transformation. It starts with small, intentional choices—like mindful eating, setting health boundaries, or running with an open heart—that build on each other over time. If you find yourself always giving, always doing, without pausing to fill your own cup, ask yourself: What's one small way I can start showing love to myself today? These small steps may seem simple, but they can have a profound effect, creating a ripple of positive change that touches every corner of your life.

So, take a deep breath and choose one small act that honors you, and see where it leads. The path to inner love isn't about making huge leaps, but about taking small steps that bring you back to yourself. As you continue through this book, let Mike's story serve as a reminder and inspiration to start your own journey. It begins with a single decision to be kind to yourself, and from that simple choice, anything becomes possible.

Embracing Daily Practices for Inner Love
Tips for Incorporating Daily Habits
1. **Set Reminders:** Use your phone or a planner to set reminders for your daily habits.
2. **Be Consistent:** Try to practice your habits at the same time each day to create a routine.
3. **Start Small:** Begin with one or two self-care activities and gradually incorporate more as you feel comfortable. Over time, these small, consistent actions will compound, forming lasting habits that enhance your well-being and resilience.

Reflections

Morning Reflection:

How do I feel after my morning affirmations? Am I starting my day with a positive mindset?

Evening Reflection:

What three things am I grateful for today?

How does focusing on gratitude change my perspective?

Exercise

Developing a Self-Care Routine

1. Identify Your Needs

Step 1: Assess Your Well-being

Take a moment to reflect on different areas of your life—physical, emotional, mental, and social. Ask yourself where you may need more balance and care. If you have any medical concerns, it's always best to consult a healthcare professional before making changes to your self-care routine.

1. How do I feel physically? Am I getting enough rest and nourishment?
2. How do I feel emotionally? Am I managing my stress and emotions effectively?

3. How do I feel mentally? Am I stimulating my mind and engaging in activities I enjoy?
4. How do I feel socially? Am I maintaining healthy relationships and connections?

Step 2: Prioritize Your Needs

Identify areas where you need more care and attention. For example, if you feel mentally drained, prioritize activities that stimulate your mind and bring joy.

1. Set Aside Time

Step 1: Schedule Self-Care

Allocate specific times for self-care activities in your daily or weekly schedule. Treat these appointments with yourself as non-negotiable, just like a meeting or a doctor's appointment.

Step 2: Create a Self-Care Plan

Write down your self-care activities and when you will do them. For example:

- Morning: 10 minutes of meditation
- Afternoon: 30-minute walk
- Evening: Read or listen to a book for 20 minutes

1. Choose Activities That Nourish You

Examples of Self-Care Activities:
- Physical: yoga, jogging, stretching, relaxing bath, or gym exercise
- Emotional: journaling, talking to a friend, practicing gratitude
- Mental: reading, solving puzzles, learning a new skill
- Social: spending time with loved ones, joining a club or group, volunteering

1. Be Consistent

Make self-care a regular part of your routine, not just something you do when you feel burned out. For example:
1. Incorporate 30 minutes of physical activity into your daily routine, such as a brisk walk or yoga session.
2. Choose nutritious foods that energize you, like fresh fruits, vegetables, and whole grains.
3. Plan your meals ahead to ensure a balanced diet.

Rita's Self-Care Awakening

Rita's days were a blur of to-do lists and endless responsibilities. Between managing a demanding job, caring for her two children, and supporting her aging parents, she was always on the move—

always giving, yet rarely pausing to breathe. Life felt like a relentless race against time, and she was losing—exhausted, frazzled, and increasingly disconnected from the simple joys she once cherished.

One evening, after yet another chaotic day, Rita caught a glimpse of herself in the bathroom mirror. The reflection staring back seemed like a stranger—tired eyes, slumped shoulders, and a weariness that ran deeper than physical fatigue. In that quiet moment, a thought surfaced, soft yet insistent: "What if I took some time for myself?" It wasn't about escaping her responsibilities but learning to coexist with them more peacefully.

She started small, carving out 30 minutes each evening just for herself—a sacred window of time that belonged to no one else. At first, it felt almost wrong, as if she were neglecting her duties. But she persisted, setting boundaries and resisting the familiar pull of never-ending tasks. Some nights, she lost herself in a novel, transported to distant worlds. Other times, she ran a hot bath, letting the soothing scent of lavender wrap around her like a comforting embrace. Occasionally, she simply sat in silence, allowing the quiet to unravel the knots in her mind.

Those 30 minutes became a sanctuary—a space where she could reconnect with the parts of herself buried under years of obligation and stress. The changes were subtle at first—her mood lightened, her energy renewed, her laughter more frequent. She became more present, not just with her family but with herself. The world around her hadn't changed, but how she moved through it had.

Rita's transformation rippled outward. Her husband noticed her renewed calm, her children delighted in the mother who was now more playful and less hurried, and even her colleagues remarked on the difference. She was no longer just surviving her days; she was living them, fully and with intention. The simple act of prioritizing herself had unlocked a wellspring of resilience and joy she hadn't realized she was missing.

I recall a similar moment in my own journey of self-awareness. One evening, as I sat quietly, my four-year-old daughter came close, looked into my eyes, and asked, "Dad, are you my true Dad?" I burst into laughter, initially unsure of what she meant. But upon reflection, I realized she must have sensed the shift within me—the newfound calmness, the deeper presence, the subtle yet profound transformation.

One night, as Rita soaked in her bath, her young daughter peeked in, eyes wide with curiosity. "Can I sit with you, Mom?" she asked. Rita smiled, lifting her arm to make space. In that quiet moment, she understood—this journey wasn't just hers. It was a gift she was passing on. By choosing to care for herself, she was teaching her children a powerful lesson: inner-love isn't selfish—it's essential.

Rita's journey didn't require grand gestures or drastic changes. It was the quiet, consistent choice to honor herself in the midst of life's chaos. And in doing so, she found her way back to the woman she had always been—waiting patiently beneath the surface. She was reminded that sometimes, the most profound transformations begin with the simplest steps—a few minutes of stillness, a deep breath, and the decision to finally come home to oneself.

User Testimonial

Testimonial: "Incorporating daily self-care activities into my routine has been life changing. I feel more energized, focused, and at peace. It's amazing how small changes can make such a big difference." – Michael, 35

Morning Affirmation Routine

A Morning Affirmation Routine is a consistent practice of repeating positive statements or affirmations to yourself at the beginning of each day, typically immediately after waking up. The purpose is to:

1. Self-Worth Affirmations

"I am worthy of love and respect."

"I am enough just as I am."

"I deserve happiness and success."

2. Confidence Affirmations

"I believe in my abilities."

"I am confident and self-assured."

"I can handle whatever comes my way."

3. Gratitude Affirmations

"I am grateful for my life and all its blessings."

"I appreciate the beauty in every day."

"I am thankful for the love and support in my life."

4. Positive Outlook Affirmations

"Today is going to be a great day."

"I choose to see the good in every situation."

"I embrace the opportunities that come my way."

Reflections

1. Morning Reflection

After saying your affirmations, take a moment to reflect on how they make you feel.

Example Reflection

Morning Reflection: "After saying my affirmations, I feel a surge of positivity and confidence. I feel ready to face the day with a positive mindset."

Questions to Ask

    How do I feel emotionally after my affirmations?

    Do I notice a shift in my mindset or energy?

2. Evening Reflection

At the end of the day, reflect on how your morning affirmations influenced your day.

Evening Reflection: "Throughout the day, I noticed that I was more resilient in the face of challenges. My affirmations helped me stay calm and focused, and I felt a sense of inner peace."

Questions to Ask

    Did my affirmations help me stay positive and focused?

    How did they impact my interactions and decisions?

The Power of Gratitude Journaling

Journaling is a powerful tool for processing thoughts and emotions, offering a safe space to explore your inner world without judgment. Gratitude journaling, in particular, can transform your perspective by shifting your focus from what's missing to what's already abundant in your life. This simple yet profound practice cultivates inner love, deepens appreciation, and enhances overall well-being.

Imagine ending each day with a moment of reflection, acknowledging the positive aspects of your life—no matter how small. Over time, this habit uplifts your spirit, fosters a positive outlook, and strengthens your connection with yourself. As Oprah Winfrey once said, "I always keep a gratitude journal with me."

Personally, I incorporate gratitude journaling into my morning routine—either after meditation or exercise, depending on the weather. This practice helps me stay grounded, fostering a sense of calm and grace as I move through the day.

James's Journey to Inner Love Through Gratitude Journaling

James often felt overwhelmed by the relentless demands of daily life. With responsibilities piling up and an ever-present sense of unease, he found himself caught in a whirlwind of stress. Each day blurred into the next, defined by a cycle of negativity that seemed impossible to break. The more he focused on his problems, the more trapped he felt, weighed down by the pressures of it all.

One evening, in an attempt to distract himself, James mindlessly scrolled through Facebook. Amid the endless posts, he came across a self-improvement page he had followed months ago. A particular post caught his eye—it spoke about gratitude journaling, a simple practice of writing down three things you're grateful for each day. The post was filled with testimonials from people who had transformed their outlook on life through this daily habit. At first, James was skeptical. Could something so simple really make a difference? Yet, a quiet voice inside urged him to give it a try.

The next morning, James picked up an old notebook, sat down, and wrote his first three entries: a sunny morning, a call from a friend, and the comfort of his favorite meal. The exercise felt awkward, almost forced, and he questioned whether it would have any real impact. But he made a promise to himself—to keep going, even on the days when finding something positive seemed impossible.

As the days passed, something subtle yet profound began to shift. The act of consciously searching for things to be grateful for rewired his focus. He started noticing small moments of joy—a stranger's warm smile, the rich aroma of his morning coffee, the satisfaction of completing a task. The stresses of life didn't vanish, but they no longer consumed him. His perspective began to shift from what was missing to what was already present.

Weeks turned into months, and James's journal became more than just a collection of gratitude lists—it became a testament to the beauty woven into everyday life. Gratitude was no longer just a practice; it had become a way of seeing the world. He felt lighter, more resilient, and more connected to the present moment. His relationships flourished as he expressed appreciation more freely, deepening his connections and bringing more joy into his interactions.

James's story is a powerful reminder that the smallest changes can ignite the most profound transformations. By dedicating just a few moments each day to gratitude, he discovered an inner peace and fulfillment he had once thought impossible.

If you're ready to experience this shift in your own life, take that first step today. The next section will guide you in starting your own gratitude journaling practice. It's a small commitment, but as James learned, it can open the door to a life filled with joy, presence, and deeper connection. Begin your journey now—your path to greater peace starts here.

Guided Gratitude Journaling

If you're looking to deepen your gratitude practice, this activity will help you create a personalized journal—whether digital or handwritten. Customizing your journal makes it easier to stay consistent and integrate gratitude into your daily routine until it becomes a habit or a meaningful part of your ritual.

By taking just a few moments each day to reflect and document what you're grateful for, you nurture a positive mindset and build a habit that enhances your overall well-being. Ready to begin? Go ahead and create a space where gratitude can flourish!

A. Gratitude for Health

Find a comfortable position. Close your eyes, take a deep breath in, and then exhale slowly. Allow yourself to relax and settle into the present moment. Continue to breathe deeply and evenly. As you maintain your steady breathing, gently shift your focus to your body. Feel the weight of your body on the chair or floor and notice any sensations.

1. **Gratitude for Your Body:** Reflect on your body, acknowledging its strength and resilience.

"Today, I am grateful for my body's ability to ____ Thank you, body, for ____"

Example "Today, I am grateful for my body's ability to heal and protect me. Thank you, body, for carrying me through each day."

2. **Gratitude for Physical Health:** Think about the aspects of your health that you may take for granted.

"I am thankful for my health and the energy it gives me. I appreciate _____, _____, and _____."

Example "I am thankful for my health and the energy it gives me. I appreciate every breath, heartbeat, and step I take."

3. **Gratitude for Mental Health** Reflect on your mental health and clarity.

"I am grateful for my mental health and clarity. A moment today when I felt mentally strong, and calm was _____."

Example "I am grateful for my mental health and clarity. A moment today when I felt mentally strong, and calm was during my meditation session this morning."

B. Gratitude for Life

Sit comfortably and take a few deep breaths. Let go of any tension in your body. Close your eyes and continue to breathe deeply.
With each breath, feel yourself becoming more grounded and present. Begin to reflect on your life as a whole.

1.**Gratitude for Existence:** Contemplate the gift of life itself.
"I am grateful for the gift of life. A moment that made me feel alive today was _____."

Example "I am grateful for the gift of life. A moment that made me feel alive today was watching the sunset and feeling the evening breeze."

2. Gratitude for Experiences: Reflect on the experiences that have shaped you.
"I appreciate the experiences, both good and challenging, that have helped me become who I am today. An experience that taught me something valuable recently is _____."

Example "I appreciate the experiences, both good and challenging, that have helped me become who I am today. An experience that taught me something valuable recently is a challenging project at work that taught me patience and understanding."

D. Gratitude for Love

Close your eyes and take a deep breath, allowing yourself to settle into the present moment. As you inhale, focus on the warmth within your heart, feeling it expand with each breath. Let this warmth fill your entire being, surrounding you with love and gratitude.

With every exhale, gently release any tension, allowing your body to soften and relax. Let go of stress, doubt, or anything that no longer serves you, making space for love to flow freely within you. Breathe in love. Breathe out tension. Let gratitude fill your heart.

1. **Gratitude for Loved Ones:** Think of the people you love and those who love you.

"I am thankful for the love that surrounds me. Someone who showed me love today is _____."

Example "I am thankful for the love that surrounds me. Someone who showed me love today is my friend who called to check on me and made me feel cared for."

2.Gratitude for Inner love: Reflect on the love you have for yourself.

"I am grateful for the ability to love myself. A way I showed myself love today is _____."

Example "I am grateful for the ability to love myself. A way I showed myself love today is taking time to read a book I enjoy, nurturing my mind and soul."

E. Gratitude for a Peaceful Heart

Sit quietly, take a deep breath in, and exhale slowly. Close your eyes and feel yourself becoming calm and centered.

Focus on the rhythm of your breath. With each inhale, invite peace into your heart. With each exhale, release any stress or tension.

1.Gratitude for Inner Peace: Focus on the peace within your heart.

"I am grateful for the peace within me. A moment of peace I experienced today was _____."

Example "I am grateful for the peace within me. A moment of peace I experienced today was while meditating this morning."

2. Gratitude for Calm Moments: Reflect on moments of calm and tranquility in your life.
"I appreciate the calm moments that bring balance and clarity to my life. A calm moment I had today was _____."

Example "I appreciate the calm moments that bring balance and clarity to my life. A calm moment I had today was enjoying a quiet cup of tea in the afternoon."

F. Gratitude for Mindfulness

Find a comfortable seat, close your eyes, and take a deep breath in and out. As you breathe, let your awareness settle into the present moment. Notice the sensations in your body and the sounds around you.

1. Gratitude for the Present Moment: Bring your awareness to the present moment.
"I am grateful for this moment. I appreciate the here and now, fully experiencing _____."

Example "I am grateful for this moment. I appreciate the here and now, fully experiencing each breath and sensation."

2. **Gratitude for Awareness:** Reflect on your ability to be mindful.

"I am thankful for my awareness. Mindfulness helps me navigate life with _____."

Example "I am thankful for my awareness. Mindfulness helps me navigate life with clarity and compassion."

G. Gratitude for Attention

Sit comfortably, close your eyes, and take a few deep breaths, focusing on the rhythm of your breath. With each breath, feel your mind becoming more focused and clearer. Begin to reflect on your ability to pay attention and concentrate.

1. **Gratitude for Focus:** Think about your ability to concentrate and pay attention.

"I am grateful for my ability to focus. My attention allows me to _____."

Example "I am grateful for my ability to focus. My attention allows me to engage deeply with the world around me."

2. **Gratitude for Presence:** Reflect on the times when you have been fully present.

"I appreciate the moments of presence where I can connect fully with
_____."

Example "I appreciate the moments of presence where I can connect fully with my activities and relationships."

H. Gratitude for Being an Active Listener

Find a comfortable position, close your eyes, and take a few deep breaths, allowing your body to relax. As you inhale, tune into your inner voice and the subtle sounds around you—the rustle of leaves, the hum of distant chatter, or the rhythm of your breath. With each exhale, let go of distractions and allow yourself to become fully present in the act of listening. Embrace the gift of attentiveness, knowing that true listening deepens understanding, strengthens connections, and nurtures meaningful conversations.

1. Gratitude for Listening Skills

Think about your ability to listen actively.

"I am grateful for my ability to listen. Active listening helps me _____."

Example "I am grateful for my ability to listen. Active listening helps me understand and connect with others deeply."

2. Gratitude for Connection

Reflect on the connections you've built through listening.

"I appreciate the connections I've made through listening. My attentiveness strengthens my _____."

Example "I appreciate the connections I've made through listening. My attentiveness strengthens

My relationships and fosters mutual respect."

Additional Personalized gratitude

Examples

1. Daily Gratitude

    Today, I am grateful for.

    The warmth of the sun on my face during my morning walk.

    The delicious coffee I enjoyed with a friend.

    The supportive message I received from a colleague.

2. Weekly Gratitude

    This week, I am grateful for;

    Overcoming a difficult task at work and learning new skills.

    Spending quality time with my family and sharing laughter.

    The peaceful moments I spent reading my favorite book.

3. Monthly Gratitude

This month, I am grateful for;

The progress I made in my personal goals.

The kindness and support of my friends.

The beautiful experiences I had exploring nature.

Additional prompts to personalize your Journal

1. Daily Gratitude Prompts

What are three things you are grateful for today?

Who is someone you are thankful for, and why?

Describe a moment today that made you smile.

2. Weekly Gratitude Prompts

Reflect on a challenge you faced this week. What did you learn from it?

What is something you achieved this week that you are proud of?

Name a small thing that brought you joy this week.

3. Monthly Gratitude Prompts

What are the top three things you are grateful for this month?

How have your feelings of gratitude evolved over the month?

Reflect on a person who made a positive impact on your life this month.

Gratitude Journaling as a Lifestyle Practice

Always remember Gratitude journaling is more than just a daily habit—it's a powerful ongoing practice that, when embedded into your lifestyle, nurtures everlasting love, happiness, and peace. By consistently reflecting on the positives in your life, you cultivate a mindset of appreciation that transforms the way you experience the world around you. This journey of gratitude is a continuous path, encouraging you to savor the present, cherish meaningful connections, and build a resilient spirit. As you incorporate this practice into your daily routine, you'll find that gratitude becomes not just something you do, but a fundamental part of who you are.

CHAPTER 5

MINDFULNESS AND INNER PEACE

You're sitting in traffic, your mind racing with a thousand thoughts—work deadlines, unfinished errands, a call you forgot to return. Amidst the chaos, you spot a jogger effortlessly gliding past the cars, seemingly unbothered by the world around him. You think, how can he be so calm? That was me—constantly overwhelmed, trapped in a relentless cycle of overthinking—until I discovered the transformative power of mindfulness.

At first, I struggled. Sitting still for even a few minutes felt impossible. No matter how hard I tried, my mind would wander—pulled into past regrets or future anxieties. Focusing on the present felt frustrating and unnatural. That is, until an unexpected experience changed everything. It all started with my desire to buy the new iPhone 16. Excited, I headed to the Apple Store at Chestnut Hill Mall, only to be disappointed when I learned it was out of stock. An attendant suggested checking another location. "Could you find a nearby store that has it?" I asked. She quickly searched and informed me that the Wakefield store had one available.

Just as I turned to leave, something caught my eye—a mesmerizing display of the Vision Pro. The visuals on the screen were breathtaking, almost surreal. Lost in fascination, I barely noticed a friendly Apple staff member approaching me.

"We're launching the Vision Pro today," he said with a smile. "Would you like to try it?"

I hesitated for a moment. Then, a nearby customer, grinning, chimed in, "You should try it—it's an incredible experience."

Encouraged, I said, "Sure."

The attendant carefully calibrated the device before I placed it on my head. What happened next was nothing short of extraordinary.

The moment the Vision Pro activated, I felt as if I had stepped into another dimension. The visuals were stunningly immersive, and the intuitive hand gestures made navigation feel like something out of a sci-fi movie. Reality and fantasy coexisted seamlessly in this digital space. For the first time in a long while, I was completely present—fully engaged in the moment. The sensation was exhilarating, almost euphoric.

When I removed the headset, I was buzzing with excitement. "How much is this?" I asked eagerly.

"$3,500," the attendant replied.

I let out a low whistle. "Wow. I don't have that budget right now, but I need to get one."

As I walked out of the store, my mind was fixated on one thought: Could VR help me with mindfulness? If the Vision Pro could immerse me so completely in a digital world, could it also train my mind to stay present in the real one?

Determined to explore this idea, I started researching alternatives and came across the Meta Quest 3 at Best Buy. While it wasn't as advanced as the Vision Pro, it was a fantastic alternative—one that fit my budget. I bought it and soon discovered apps like Tripp, which transported me into breathtaking meditative landscapes. These immersive experiences helped me focus, quieting the endless stream of thoughts that had once felt uncontrollable.

Now, mindfulness is no longer a struggle—it's a journey. The same mind that once resisted stillness now craves these immersive moments of presence. Who would have thought that a simple visit to an Apple Store in search of a phone would lead me to a revolutionary way of experiencing mindfulness?

"Peace comes from within. Do not seek it without." — *Buddha*

Mindfulness is the art of being fully present—acknowledging thoughts, emotions, and sensations without judgment. It's like hitting the pause button on life's chaos and taking a moment to breathe. By fostering self-awareness, mindfulness deepens inner love. When you tune into your inner world, you become more attuned to your needs, treating yourself with the kindness and respect you deserve. This practice not only reduces stress and anxiety but also cultivates a profound sense of peace. Research by Fredrickson et al. (2008) supports this, showing that positive emotions—nurtured through inner love and mindfulness—build resilience against stress and adversity.

Why Mindfulness Matters for Inner love
Mindfulness helps you develop a compassionate relationship with yourself. It allows you to observe your thoughts and feelings without being swept away by them. This awareness is the foundation of inner love, as it encourages you to embrace your true self—flaws, strengths, and resilience. Through mindfulness, you learn to be gentle with yourself, acknowledging your humanity and cultivating a nurturing inner dialogue.

Research in positive psychology highlights that mindfulness encourages you to approach your thoughts and feelings with non-judgmental awareness, which enhances self-acceptance. For instance, a study published in *Self and Identity* found that individuals who practice mindfulness are more likely to engage in self-compassionate behaviors, leading to improved emotional well-being. By observing your internal experiences without reactivity, you nurture your inner dialogue that acknowledges both strengths and weaknesses, fostering a healthier relationship with yourself and enhancing the capacity for inner love.

Neuroimaging research has also shown that mindfulness practices can activate brain regions associated with self-referential processing and emotional regulation, such as the medial prefrontal cortex and the insula. This suggests that mindfulness not only enhances emotional awareness but also helps you to create a compassionate relationship with yourself. By fostering a sense of acceptance and reducing negative self-judgment, you facilitate a deeper connection to inner love and self-worth

Four Main Mindfulness Practices to Enhance Self-Awareness and Inner Peace

PRACTICE 1: Mindful Breathing

Mindful breathing is a simple yet powerful practice that anchors you in the present moment. It helps calm your mind, reduces stress, and enhances focus, creating a deep sense of inner peace. Whether you're starting your day, taking a break, or unwinding in the evening, mindful breathing can bring clarity and relaxation. Personally, on particularly busy days when I don't have time to go for a run or workout, I rely on guided breathing exercises using tools like the TRIPP App on the Meta Quest 3. These mindful exercises help improve my focus, boost productivity, and sometimes even create a free-flowing feeling of love and presence.

For beginners, these sensations might not be immediately noticeable. However, with practice, discipline, consistency, and improved focus, you may begin to experience a shift—feeling lighter, more aware, and more attuned to your emotions and surroundings. Over time, this practice can elevate your mood and cultivate an awakened sense of mindfulness throughout your day.

Step-by-Step Guided mindful Breathing Practice

Step 1: Find a Comfortable Position
- a) Choose a quiet place where you won't be disturbed.
- b) Sit upright with your back straight or lie down comfortably with your arms relaxed by your sides.

    c) Gently close your eyes and take a few deep breaths to settle in.

    d) Allow your body to relax, releasing any tension with each exhale.

Step 2: Focus on Your Breath

    a) Shift your attention to the natural rhythm of your inhales and exhales.

    b) Observe the cool sensation of air entering your nostrils and the warm sensation as you exhale.

    c) Feel the rise and fall of your chest or the expansion and contraction of your abdomen with each breath.

    d) Allow yourself to be fully present, letting go of distractions.

Step 3: Breathe Naturally

    a) Let your breath flow effortlessly without trying to control it.

    b) If your breath feels shallow or uneven, simply observe without judgment—it will naturally find its rhythm.

    c) Embrace a sense of ease and surrender as you focus on the act of breathing.

Step 4: Count Your Breaths (Optional)

a) If staying focused feels challenging, try using a breath-counting technique:
b) Inhale and silently count "one", exhale and count "two".
c) Continue this pattern up to ten, then restart from one.
d) If you lose track, gently begin again. The goal is presence, not perfection.

Step 5: Return to Your Breath
a) If your mind wanders, acknowledge the thoughts without judgment and gently return to your breath.
b) View distractions as opportunities to strengthen your focus.
c) Continue this practice for 5-10 minutes, gradually increasing the time as you become more comfortable.

With regular practice, mindful breathing will enhance your awareness, improves emotional regulation, and creates lasting inner balance. Breathe with intention, stay present, and embrace the peace that flows with each inhale and exhale.

Benefits of Mindful breathing

1. Reduces Stress and Anxiety

Focusing on your breath calms the mind and lowers the production of stress hormones like cortisol, helping you feel more grounded and at ease.

2. Improves Focus and Concentration

Regular practice enhances your ability to stay present, sharpen your attention, and improve cognitive performance.

3. Enhances Emotional Regulation

Mindful breathing increases self-awareness, allowing you to recognize and manage emotions more effectively, fostering emotional balance.

4. Promotes Deep Relaxation

By activating the parasympathetic nervous system, mindful breathing encourages a state of calm, helping the body and mind unwind.

PRACTICE 2: Mindful Eating

Mindful eating is the practice of fully engaging with the experience of eating, using all your senses to savor each bite. It fosters a healthier relationship with food and helps you become more attuned to your body's needs. When you eat with awareness, you start to notice how your body communicates—what it craves, what nourishes it, and what it rejects.

Children naturally embody this mindfulness. They eat with curiosity, playfulness, and full engagement. I often observe this with my three-year-old daughter. When I give her food, she doesn't just eat—she explores. She stares at it, examines it, and asks questions with genuine curiosity:

"Why is this chocolate black when yesterday we had a brown one?"

"Why is this chocolate bitter when yesterday it was sweet?"

"Why this? Why that?"

At first, I found her endless questions overwhelming. But as I deepened my own mindfulness practice, I began to see them as a source of power—a reflection of presence, curiosity, and an eagerness to learn. Now, I welcome every question, no matter how small, because I understand that mindfulness begins with awareness and inquiry.

Mindful eating is not just about what we consume but how we experience it. When we slow down, engage our senses, and listen to our bodies, we cultivate a deeper connection with food, our emotions, and the present moment.

Exercise: The Mindful Eating

1. Choose a small piece of food—like a raisin or a piece of chocolate.

   I choose a _____

2. Before eating, observe the food. Notice its color, texture, and shape.

   I observe the _____ of the food. It is _____ in color, has a _____ texture, and is _____ in shape.

3. Bring the food to your nose and take in its aroma.

   I bring the _____ to my nose and notice its aroma, which smells _____

4. Slowly place the food in your mouth but pause before chewing. Take a moment to notice its texture, temperature, and how it feels on your tongue.

   I slowly place this _____ in my mouth. On my tongue, it feels _____.

5. Begin to chew slowly, paying attention to the taste and texture.

I begin to chew slowly, paying attention to the _____ taste and _____ texture.

6. Focus on the act of eating, experiencing each moment fully.

    I focus on the act of eating, experiencing the _____ and _____ of each moment.

7. Swallow the food and take a moment to reflect on the experience.

    I swallow the _____ and take a moment to reflect on the experience. I feel _____ and _____

PRACTICE 3: Walking Meditation

Walking meditation combines movement with mindfulness, helping you cultivate awareness and inner peace while being active.

Exercise: The Walking Meditation

1. Find a quiet place where you can walk without distractions.
2. Stand still for a moment and take a few deep breaths.
3. Begin to walk slowly, paying attention to the sensation of your feet touching the ground.
4. Notice the rhythm of your steps, the movement of your legs, and the balance of your body.
5. If your mind starts to wander, gently bring your focus back to the physical sensations of walking.

6. Continue walking for 10-15 minutes, gradually increasing the time as you become more comfortable with the practice.

PRACTICE 4: Body Scan Meditation

As discussed in Chapter 3, body scan meditation is a powerful practice that increases awareness of physical sensations, promotes relaxation, and enhances self-awareness. By tuning into different parts of your body, you can release tension and cultivate a deeper connection with yourself. For a guided practice, revisit Chapter 3 and follow the steps to experience the full benefits of body scan meditation.

Overcoming Self-Criticism with Mindfulness

Hannah had always been her own harshest critic. Despite countless accomplishments, a relentless inner voice constantly whispered, "You're not good enough." Every mistake, no matter how small, fueled her self-doubt. The weight of her self-criticism overshadowed even her greatest successes, casting a cloud of negativity over her life.

One gray afternoon, as rain tapped softly against her office window, Hannah sat motionless at her desk, staring blankly at her computer screen. She had just received feedback on a project she had poured her heart into. While the critique was largely constructive, all she could focus on were the areas for improvement.

"I should have done better," she thought as her chest tightened. "Why can't I ever get it right?"

Overwhelmed, she decided to take a walk to clear her mind. Without a destination in mind, she wandered through the city streets until she found herself standing outside a small, serene bookstore. The warm light inside beckoned her, and she drifted in, browsing the shelves aimlessly. Then a book caught her eye: The Art of Mindfulness.

Drawn to its simplicity, she picked it up and began flipping through the pages. Phrases like "observe without judgment" and "embrace the present moment" resonated deeply with her. She realized how often she was lost in her thoughts, missing the world around her while trapped in endless loops of self-criticism.

"Maybe this is what I need," she thought, her curiosity piqued."

That evening, curled up in her favorite armchair, Hannah began reading. The book described mindfulness as a way of living in the present, of observing one's thoughts and emotions without judging them as good or bad. It was a revelation—perhaps, for the first time, she realized that her thoughts didn't have to define her reality.

The next morning, Hannah decided to give mindfulness a try. Sitting on her balcony, she closed her eyes and focused on her breathing. Almost immediately, her mind began to wander, pulling her into a familiar swirl of thoughts.

"You're wasting time. This won't help. You have so much to do." The urge to abandon the practice was strong, but she remembered the book's advice: "Notice your thoughts, then let them pass like clouds in the sky." With patience, she visualized each critical thought drifting away, making space for something softer. Slowly, a sense of calm washed over her.

Days turned into weeks, and Hannah consistently maintained her new daily practice. One afternoon at work, she made a significant error in a report—something that would have once sent her spiraling into self-doubt.

"How could I be so careless?" she thought, her familiar self-criticism rising. But this time, she paused, took a deep breath, and reframed the situation.

> "I made a mistake, but that's okay. I can fix it."
> *"Mindfulness means being awake. It means knowing what you are doing." – Jon Kabat-Zinn*

It was a small shift, but it made a world of difference. Instead of drowning in negativity, she addressed the error calmly and moved forward with her day. One evening, over dinner with her close friend Mia, Hannah opened up about her mindfulness journey.

"I've noticed you seem more at peace lately," Mia said, sipping her tea. "What's changed?"

Hannah smiled. "I've been practicing mindfulness," she explained. "It's helping me be kinder to myself."

"That's wonderful," Mia replied. "Do you find it difficult?"

"At first, yes," Hannah admitted. "My mind was always racing. But now, it's like I've found this quiet space within myself. I'm learning to accept my thoughts and let them go without attaching to them."

As they parted, Mia hugged her warmly. "I'm so happy for you. You deserve that peace."

Later that night, Hannah reflected on her progress. She no longer felt imprisoned by her self-critical thoughts, and her growing inner love was manifesting outwardly in ways others, like Mia, were beginning to notice.

Sitting on her bed, she pulled out her journal, breathed gently, and wrote:

"Today, I choose to be gentle with myself. I acknowledge my imperfections and embrace them as part of my journey."

She closed the journal, feeling warmth spread through her heart. For the first time in a long while, she looked forward to the future with hope rather than fear.

Hannah's story is a powerful reminder of how mindfulness can transform the way we relate to ourselves. If you've been caught in the cycle of self-criticism, let her journey inspire you to take that first step. Start small—just a few minutes a day—creating space to observe your thoughts without judgment. Be patient and gentle with yourself, understanding that mindfulness is a continuous practice, not a one-time fix.

In the next section, you'll find guided meditations designed to help you connect with your inner peace and nurture self-love. Allow these practices to guide you on your journey inward, where true transformation begins and then radiates outward.

Loving-Kindness Meditation

Loving-kindness meditation, also known as Metta meditation, involves directing positive energy and wishes towards yourself and others. It fosters compassion and inner love.

Exercise: The Loving-Kindness Meditation Guide
 1. Find a comfortable seated position and close your eyes.
 2. Take a few deep breaths, allowing yourself to relax.

3. Begin by focusing on yourself.

Silently repeat the following phrases:

"I am happy."

"I am healthy."

"I am safe."

"I am at peace"

"I am wealthy of love"

"I am loving awareness"

"I live with ease."

"I am………………"

    3. After a few minutes, bring to mind someone you care about and repeat the phrases for them:

"You are at peace"

"You are loving awareness "

"You are happy."

"You are healthy."

"You are safe."

"You live with ease."

"You are……………"

5. Gradually extend these wishes to others in your life, including neutral people and even those you find challenging.

6. Finish by extending these wishes to all beings everywhere:

    "All beings live with happiness."

    "All beings deserve health."

"All beings deserve safety."

"All beings live with ease."

"All beings deserve _____"

Building Self-Compassion through Meditation

Jackson often felt like he was at the mercy of his emotions. Waves of anger, frustration, and sadness would crash over him without warning, leaving him reacting impulsively and regretting his actions later. He found himself caught in a cycle of emotional overwhelm, unable to break free from the grip of his reactions. He longed for a way to regain control, to feel more at peace with himself, but didn't know where to begin.

One evening, while browsing through self-improvement videos on YouTube, Jackson accidentally stumbled upon a meditation guru. The video wasn't what he was initially looking for, but something about the calm demeanor of the speaker caught his attention. The guru spoke about the power of meditation—not as a quick fix, but as a daily practice that could help you become more aware of your thoughts and emotions. Intrigued by the promise of a calmer mind, Jackson decided to give it a try. He figured he had nothing to lose, and maybe—just maybe—this could be the change he was searching for.

He started small, following along with a simple guided meditation. At first, sitting still felt awkward, and his mind wandered constantly, racing through thoughts and worries. But the guru's gentle voice reminded him that it was okay, that meditation wasn't about having a perfectly clear mind, but about noticing when his thoughts strayed and gently guiding his attention back to the breath. Jackson found comfort in this permission to simply be, without judgment.

As Jackson continued to meditate, something remarkable began to happen. He learned to pause in moments of emotional intensity, to observe his feelings instead of immediately reacting. For the first time, he felt a sense of control over his responses. The space between his emotions and his actions grew, and within that space, Jackson discovered the power to choose how he wanted to respond. He found that he could meet his emotions with curiosity rather than resistance, allowing them to pass without letting them dictate his behavior.

This newfound awareness didn't just change how Jackson responded to the world; it changed how he treated himself. He started to recognize the patterns of self-criticism that had fueled his impulsivity, and he began to replace harsh judgments with self-compassion. When he made mistakes, instead of spiraling into guilt, he allowed himself to learn and grow from the experience. Meditation became more than a practice; it became a way of life, one that nurtured his inner peace and helped him build a more compassionate relationship with himself.

> *"You yourself, as much as anybody in the entire universe, deserve your love and affection." – Buddha*

Jackson's journey is a testament to the transformative power of meditation. If you've been struggling with overwhelming emotions or find yourself reacting in ways that don't serve you, consider taking a page from Jackson's story. Start small—find a quiet space, close your eyes, and focus on your breath. It may feel strange at first, but with time, you'll discover the power of pausing, the strength in stillness, and the profound impact of simply being present with yourself.

The next time you're overwhelmed, remember that you have the choice to pause, breathe, and respond with compassion. Let Jackson's story inspires you to explore meditation as a path to self-compassion and inner peace.

Self-Compassion Meditation

This meditation helps cultivate a compassionate and kind attitude towards yourself, especially during difficult times.

Exercise: The Self-Compassion Meditation

1. Sit comfortably and close your eyes.
2. Take a few deep breaths to center yourself.
3. Bring to mind a situation that is causing you stress or discomfort.
4. Place your hand over your heart and acknowledge the difficulty with kindness.

5. Silently repeat the following phrases, focusing your awareness on transcending suffering and embracing the realm of pure love. If emotional distress arises, gently bring your attention back to the present moment.

"This is a moment of suffering."

"Suffering is a part of life."

"May I be kind to myself."

"May I give myself the compassion I need."

6. Spend a few minutes repeating these phrases, allowing yourself to feel the warmth and kindness they bring.

7. Finish by taking a few deep breaths and gently opening your eyes.

PERSONAL REFLECTIONS

1: Mindful Breathing

Practicing mindful breathing has become a cornerstone of my daily routine, helping me start the day with a sense of calm and clarity. Whenever I feel stressed or overwhelmed, taking a few moments to focus on my breath brings me back to the present moment, easing my anxiety.

2: Body Scan Meditation

Body scan meditation has made me more aware of the tension I hold in my body. By regularly scanning and relaxing each part, I've learned to release stress I didn't even know I was carrying. It's like giving my body a mini vacation, leaving me feeling refreshed and at peace.

3: Mindful Walking

Mindful walking has transformed my daily walks into a meditative experience. Paying attention to each step and the sensation in my body connects me deeply to the present moment. It's a simple practice that brings profound peace and joy.

Connection Between Mindfulness and inner Love

Mindfulness and inner love are deeply interconnected. Mindfulness involves being present and fully engaged with the here and now, without judgment. It cultivates a sense of awareness and acceptance, which is essential for inner love. By practicing mindfulness, you learn to observe your thoughts and feelings without being overwhelmed by them, creating a space for self-compassion and self-acceptance.

Below are the four core principles that illustrate the connection between mindfulness and inner love.

1. **Increased Self-Awareness:** Mindfulness helps you become more aware of your thoughts, emotions, and behaviors. This awareness is the first step towards understanding and loving yourself.

2. **Reduced Self-Criticism:** By observing your thoughts without judgment, mindfulness reduces the harsh self-criticism that can erode inner love.

3. **Enhanced Emotional Regulation**: Mindfulness helps you manage your emotions more effectively, leading to greater emotional stability and resilience.

4. **Improved Self-Compassion:** Mindfulness fosters a kind and gentle attitude towards yourself, promoting self-compassion and acceptance.

Mindful Breathing
Ella's Experience with Mindful Breathing

Ella's life was a relentless whirlwind—an endless blur of deadlines, meetings, and a to-do list that seemed to grow faster than she could check things off. Each day felt like a race against time, with pressure mounting like a heavy weight on her chest. No matter how much she accomplished, there was always something more, pulling her deeper into a cycle of exhaustion and overwhelm. She longed for a sense of calm—a moment to simply breathe—but she was trapped in a life that refused to slow down. She didn't know how to find stillness in the storm.

One evening, as she mindlessly scrolled through Instagram, trying to numb herself from the day's chaos, Ella stumbled upon a video by a wellness influencer she had never seen before. The woman spoke softly but with a conviction that cut through the noise: "Mindful breathing," she said, "is not about controlling your world. It's about finding your breath when the world spins out of control." The words struck a chord deep within Ella. She realized she had been holding her breath—physically tightening her chest with each new task, and emotionally bracing for impact with every twist of her hectic life.

Desperate for a change, Ella decided to try mindful breathing, despite her skepticism. She started small, dedicating just a few minutes each morning to sitting quietly, closing her eyes, and focusing solely on the rise and fall of her breath. At first, it was almost unbearable. Her mind was a battleground of racing thoughts: unfinished emails, meetings yet to be scheduled, the endless list of things she "should" be doing. But she remembered the influencer's gentle reminder: "Be patient. Your mind will wander. Just bring it back to the breath, again and again."

Breath by breath, day by day, Ella's practice began to sink in, like roots anchoring her in a new, more solid ground. She noticed tiny shifts—glimmers of peace amidst the chaos, a feeling of being centered even when the world around her was not. As the weeks went on, those moments of stillness stretched longer and began to weave through her day. Mindful breathing became more than a morning ritual; it became a lifeline—a steady anchor that held her firm when everything else tried to pull her under.

What began as a tentative experiment blossomed into a quiet revolution within her. She found herself more present in conversations, more resilient in moments of stress, and more forgiving of herself when things didn't go according to plan. She discovered that mindful breathing wasn't about emptying her mind of thoughts, but about creating space to breathe through the noise, the mess, and the madness of everyday life.

Breath became her refuge, her sanctuary in the storm. Instead of being overwhelmed by the chaos of her days, Ella learned to pause in those critical moments—to breathe in deeply, feeling the air fill her lungs, and to release the tension with each exhale. The practice didn't erase her stress; it transformed her response to it. In the stillness of her breath, she found a power she never knew she had—the power to reclaim her peace, even when everything around her felt like it was falling apart.

Ella's journey is a soul-stirring reminder that sometimes the most profound changes come from the simplest practices. If you, too, feel overwhelmed by the demands of life, let Ella's experience be a guide. Start with just a few minutes each day. Close your eyes, breathe in deeply, and let each exhale carry away a little bit of the weight you've been holding onto.

You don't need a perfect setting or a quiet room—you only need your breath and the courage to be present with it. In the next section, you'll find a guided mindful breathing exercise that can easily fit into your daily routine. This simple yet powerful practice can help you find your own sense of calm amidst the chaos, one breath at a time. Get ready to embrace the stillness within and connect with a peace that is yours to claim, in every moment, with every breath.

CHAPTER 6

HEALING PAST WOUNDS

Techniques for Healing Emotional and Psychological Wounds

The Weight of the Past.
Imagine carrying a heavy backpack filled with rocks. Each rock represents a painful experience, a regret, or an unresolved emotion. As time goes by, the weight becomes unbearable, slowing you down and draining your energy. This was my life for many years, burdened by past wounds that I didn't know how to heal. It wasn't until I learned to unpack this emotional baggage that I felt the freedom and lightness of inner love.

"The wound is the place where the Light enters you." – Rumi
Healing emotional and psychological wounds is crucial for cultivating inner love. It involves confronting painful memories, processing emotions, and finding ways to move forward.

Here are five techniques to guide you through this healing journey.

1. Acknowledge and Accept Your Emotions

The first step in healing is to acknowledge and accept your emotions. Too often, we suppress or ignore painful feelings, hoping they will disappear. However, unprocessed emotions don't disappear—they linger, often resurfacing in ways that can be overwhelming or harmful. As the saying goes, "What you resist, persists." Instead of pushing emotions away, welcome them with awareness. Pay attention to what triggers them and recognize any patterns that emerge. By embracing your emotions rather than avoiding them, you create space for healing, growth, and self-understanding.

Exercise: The Emotional Check-In
1. Find a quiet space where you won't be disturbed.
2. Sit comfortably and take a few deep breaths to center your awareness in one place, you can put your hands in your chest.
3. Reflect on your current emotional state. Take a moment to pause and ask yourself, "What am I feeling right now?" Sit in silence and listen to your inner voice without judgment. Allow your emotions to surface naturally—without trying to rationalize or suppress them.
4. Write down your emotions without judgment. Accept and welcome them as they are, even if they are uncomfortable.
5. Spend a few minutes sitting with these emotions, allowing yourself to fully experience them.

2. Seek Professional Help

Sometimes, the wounds we carry are too deep to heal on our own. Seeking help from a therapist or counselor can provide the support and tools needed to navigate complex emotions and experiences.

3. Practice Self-Compassion

Self-compassion involves treating yourself with the same kindness and understanding that you would offer a friend. It's about recognizing your suffering and responding with care rather than criticism.

Exercise: The Self-Compassion Letter
Refill in The Self-Compassion letter below

Dear [*Your Name*],

I know that you are feeling [*emotion*] right now because of [*situation*]. It's understandable to feel this way, given everything that has happened. You might be thinking that you should have [*action*] or perhaps wishing you had [*different outcome*]. It's okay to have these thoughts and feelings. They are a natural part of processing what you've been through.

It's important to remind yourself that you have always been [*positive quality*]. This situation does not define you. You are so much more than this moment of [*difficulty/pain*]. Remember that pain is a part of growth. It's through these challenging times that you learn the most about yourself and develop your inner strength. Embrace [*difficulty/pain*], because it is helping you become the person you are meant to be. You are strong, capable, and deserving of love and happiness.

With compassion and understanding,

[*Your Name*]

Note: Read the letter aloud to yourself, allowing its compassion and kindness to resonate within you. If possible, scan the letter and email it to yourself as a reminder of the love and encouragement it holds.

4. Engage in Creative Expression

Creative activities like writing, painting, or playing music can be powerful outlets for processing and expressing emotions. They allow you to explore your feelings in a non-verbal way, providing relief and insight.

Exercise: Art Journaling

1. Gather some art supplies—markers, colored pencils, paint, or whatever you prefer.
2. Choose a quiet space where you can work without interruptions.

3. Reflect on a past wound or emotional experience.
4. Express your feelings through art. Don't worry about creating something "beautiful" or "perfect." Focus on the process and what it brings up for you.
5. After finishing, take a moment to reflect on your creation and what it reveals about your emotions.

5. Practice Mindfulness and Meditation

As discussed in the previous chapter, mindfulness and meditation help you stay present and grounded, making it easier to process difficult emotions. These practices encourage self-awareness and acceptance, both essential for healing and emotional resilience. By regularly engaging in mindfulness and meditation, you create a space for inner peace, clarity, and self-compassion.

Exercise: The Healing Breath Meditation
1. Find a comfortable place to sit or lie down.
2. Close your eyes and take a few deep breaths.
3. As you breathe in, imagine drawing healing energy into your body.
4. As you breathe out, imagine releasing pain and negativity.
5. Continue this pattern for several minutes, focusing on the sensation of healing with each breath. If you have ever

experienced love—whether through an intimate connection or the fulfillment of a passion—bring your awareness to that feeling. Allow its warmth and energy to flow through you. This is the power of energy transmutation—the ability to transform emotions, redirecting them into healing, creativity, and inner strength.

Therapy as a Healing Tool

David had always prided himself on being strong and independent, but after experiencing a traumatic event, his world turned upside down. Anxiety and depression became his constant companions, shadowing every aspect of his life. He tried everything he could think of—self-help books, meditation, even journaling—but nothing seemed to lift the heavy cloud that hung over him. Every day felt like a struggle just to get out of bed, and he began to lose hope that things would ever get better.

One late night, as he aimlessly scrolled through social media looking for a distraction, David stumbled upon a post from someone sharing their journey with therapy. The post was raw and honest, describing how seeking professional help had been a turning point in their battle with mental health. It wasn't the polished, perfect image David often saw on social media; it was real, relatable, and it struck a chord deep within him. For the first time, he considered that maybe he didn't have to go through this alone.

Intrigued but hesitant, David clicked on the video linked in the post. It was a heartfelt message from a therapist who spoke directly to those who felt overwhelmed, lost, or stuck. The therapist explained how seeking help wasn't a sign of weakness, but a courageous step toward healing. The words resonated with David, stirring something inside him that he hadn't felt in a long time: hope. The idea of therapy felt intimidating, but the more he listened, the more he realized that it might be exactly what he needed.

The next morning, David took a deep breath and made a decision. He searched for therapists in his area and scheduled his first appointment. Walking into the office felt daunting, but the therapist's warm demeanor quickly put him at ease. For the first time in a long time, David felt heard. He didn't have to pretend everything was fine or carry the burden alone. The therapist helped him navigate through his trauma, offering him coping strategies that began to make the unmanageable feel manageable.

Week by week, David noticed small shifts. He learned to confront his fears, to process his emotions without judgment, and to be kinder to himself. Therapy wasn't an instant fix, but it became a safe space where he could unpack his pain and rebuild his strength.

Slowly, the overwhelming weight of anxiety and depression began to lift. David started to feel more like himself again—stronger, more resilient, and better equipped to handle life's challenges.

David's journey is a powerful reminder that you don't have to face your struggles alone. If you're feeling overwhelmed, lost, or stuck, consider taking a step toward therapy. It's okay to seek help, and it's okay to need support. You deserve to be heard, and you deserve to heal. Reach out, schedule that first appointment, and open the door to the possibility of change. Therapy can be a transformative tool in your healing journey, helping you navigate life's challenges with renewed strength and hope.

The Role of Forgiveness in Inner love
Letting Go of the Past
Forgiveness is a vital part of healing past wounds and cultivating inner love. It requires releasing resentment, anger, and the desire for revenge, not as a way of excusing the harm done but as a means of freeing yourself from its emotional weight. True forgiveness isn't about simply saying the words—it's about the emotional relief and liberation it brings. I vividly remember a friend who once came to me seeking forgiveness. Her words were sincere, yet her tone and demeanor didn't align with them. It was a reminder that forgiveness

is not just about what is said, but about what is felt—both by the one offering it and the one receiving it. Letting go of the past doesn't mean forgetting; it means choosing peace over pain and allowing yourself to move forward with a lighter heart.

Embracing Your Humanity

Forgiving yourself is just as important as forgiving others. We all make mistakes and have regrets, but self-forgiveness involves recognizing your humanity and showing yourself compassion.

A powerful practice for cultivating forgiveness is Ho'oponopono, an ancient Hawaiian mantra popularized by Dr. Ihaleakala Hew Len, a Hawaiian psychologist and spiritual teacher. He used this method to heal himself and others, demonstrating how self-cleansing can transform both our inner and outer world. The mantra goes:

"I'm sorry, please forgive me, thank you, I love you."

These simple yet profound words serve as a reminder to acknowledge our imperfections, take responsibility for our experiences, and open our hearts to healing. When practiced regularly, Ho'oponopono can help release guilt, foster inner-love, and create a deeper sense of inner peace.

Exercise

The Forgiveness Meditation

1. Sit comfortably and close your eyes.
2. Take a few deep breaths to center yourself.
3. Recall someone you need to forgive, whether it's yourself or someone else.
4. Silently repeat the following phrases:

    "I forgive you for any pain you have caused."

    "May you be happy, healthy, and free."

    "I release the hold this pain has on me."

5. Spend a few minutes repeating these phrases, focusing on the feelings of release and peace they bring. Remember, the goal is not to relive emotions of pain or guilt, but to find peace in life's uncertainties and mysteries. As the saying goes, all relationships have a beginning, middle, and end. Instead of dwelling on what was lost, shift your focus to the experiences that brought you joy and moments of triumph. In doing so, you will uncover the peace and love that still exist within you.

The Power of Forgiveness

Maria had been carrying the heavy burden of resentment for years. A deep wound inflicted by a family member left her feeling betrayed and angry. Bitterness seeped into every corner of her life, affecting her relationships, health, and sense of peace. She tried to push the feelings aside, but the anger lingered, simmering just beneath the surface.

Hoping to find relief, Maria moved from one church to another, seeking solace in sermons and prayers. Yet, each experience provided only temporary relief, never truly lifting the weight from her heart. It felt like a chain binding her to the past, preventing her from fully embracing the present. One afternoon, while browsing through a bookstore, Maria picked up a book on personal development. She felt an inexplicable pull toward a chapter on forgiveness. It seemed ironic—why should she let go of something that had caused her so much pain? "Forgiveness feels impossible," she thought. But as she read, something shifted.

The book described forgiveness not as a favor to the one who caused harm, but as a gift to oneself—a way to release pain and free the heart. The author spoke of forgiveness as a powerful act of self-liberation, a process of letting go that could lead to deep healing. The words resonated deeply. Maria realized that her resentment wasn't punishing the other person—it was punishing her. Holding onto anger was like drinking poison and expecting the other person to suffer. For the first time, she considered that forgiveness might be the key to her own healing. Determined to change, Maria purchased the book and embarked on a journey of forgiveness. It wasn't easy, and it didn't happen overnight. She started small, practicing meditation and self-reflection. Each day, she sat quietly, allowing herself to feel the emotions she had buried for so long. Slowly, with each exhale, she released them—bit by bit. She visualized the weight of resentment dissolving, freeing her from its grip.

As the days passed, Maria noticed a profound change within herself. The tightness in her chest eased, and her mind became less clouded by anger. She realized that forgiveness wasn't about condoning the past or forgetting what happened—it was about choosing freedom over pain. It was about reclaiming her power and taking back control of her peace. With time, Maria felt lighter, as if a weight had been lifted from her shoulders. Her relationships improved—no longer burdened by unresolved pain, she was able to connect with others from a place of love rather than resentment. But most importantly, she felt a deep sense of inner peace, a quiet strength that allowed her to move forward with grace and an open heart.

Maria's journey teaches us that forgiveness is not about the other person—it is about setting yourself free. If you are holding onto anger or resentment, consider that forgiveness might be the key to your own healing. It is not about forgetting or excusing the past but about releasing its hold on you. Take a lesson from Maria's story. Start small—whether through meditation, journaling, or simply reflecting on your emotions. Allow yourself to begin the process of letting go at your own pace. Forgiveness is a journey, not a destination, and every step forward is a step toward reclaiming your peace. Your heart deserves to be free—let the power of forgiveness guides you there.

Tom's Path to Forgiveness

Tom had spent most of his life harboring deep resentment towards his father, who had abandoned their family when he was just a child. The anger he felt was like a shadow that followed him everywhere, seeping into his relationships, clouding his judgment, and weighing heavily on his mental health. He tried to bury the pain, but no matter how much he ignored it, the wound never truly healed. It felt like a part of him was forever stuck in that moment of abandonment, unable to move forward.

One evening, while browsing through self-improvement videos on YouTube, Tom stumbled upon a video by an influencer who spoke candidly about the power of forgiveness. The influencer shared their own story of overcoming deep-seated anger and finding peace through forgiveness, not as a way to condone the actions of those who hurt them, but as a means to free themselves from the chains of the past. Tom wasn't expecting to be moved, but something about the message resonated deeply. It was as if the influencer was speaking directly to him, offering a glimpse of a different path—one that didn't involve carrying the heavy burden of anger any longer.

Inspired by the video, Tom decided it was time to take action. He knew forgiveness wouldn't come easily, but he was willing to try. He started with meditation, using it as a tool to quiet his mind and explore his feelings without judgment. The practice allowed him to sit with his pain, to acknowledge the hurt that he had tried so hard to suppress. Through meditation, he began to realize that his anger, while justified, was also holding him back from living a full and happy life.

Tom also took to writing letters to his father—letters filled with everything he wished he could say but never had the chance to. He poured out his anger, his hurt, and his longing for closure. He didn't send these letters; instead, they became a private outlet for him to express the emotions that had been locked away for so long. Each letter was like a piece of the heavy armor he had built around his heart, slowly being removed.

Recognizing that he couldn't do it alone, Tom also sought the guidance of a therapist. Together, they explored the roots of his anger and worked on strategies to let go of the resentment that had defined so much of his life. The therapist helped him understand that forgiveness wasn't about excusing his father's actions or pretending the pain didn't exist—it was about releasing the hold that pain had on him. It was about choosing to heal for his own sake.

Over time, Tom's anger began to diminish. It didn't happen overnight, and there were moments when the old feelings would resurface. But each time, Tom chose to return to his practices—his meditation, his letters, his therapy sessions—and little by little, he felt a shift within. The resentment that had once consumed him was gradually replaced by a sense of peace. Forgiving his father didn't erase the past, but it allowed Tom to release the emotional burden he had carried for so long. He realized that holding onto anger was like keeping himself locked in a prison of his own making, and forgiveness was the key to setting himself free.

Tom's journey to forgiveness is a powerful reminder that letting go of the past doesn't mean forgetting—it means choosing to no longer let it define you. If you're struggling with resentment or unresolved anger, consider taking a page from Tom's story. Explore what forgiveness could look like for you. Start with small steps—whether it's through meditation, writing, or seeking professional support.

Remember, forgiveness isn't about the person who hurt you; it's about reclaiming your peace. Take the first step and allow yourself the freedom to heal. Your journey to forgiveness may not be easy, but it's a path that leads to a lighter heart and a more fulfilled life.

Evelyn's Creative Healing

Evelyn's world was shattered when she lost someone she deeply loved. The grief was overwhelming—like a heavy fog that refused to lift, obscuring any sense of direction. Each day felt like a struggle, and the weight of her loss seemed insurmountable. She went through the motions of daily life, but her heart wasn't in it. She felt stuck, unable to move forward, and uncertain about how to begin healing. One restless night, in an attempt to distract herself, Evelyn found herself scrolling through social media reels. As she mindlessly swiped through videos, she stumbled upon a clip from a recovery coach discussing the power of creative healing—the idea of using art to express emotions too deep for words, a way to honor both the pain and the love that come with loss. The concept resonated with Evelyn. It felt like an invitation to explore her grief rather than suppress it.

Inspired by the coach's words, Evelyn decided to pick up a paintbrush for the first time in years. She spread out a canvas and began to paint, not with the intention of creating something perfect, but simply to let her emotions flow. The colors and shapes became an extension of her inner world—each stroke reflecting her sorrow, memories, and the love she still carried. Through art, Evelyn found a way to express the emotions she had been holding inside. As she continued painting, Evelyn noticed a shift within herself. The act of creating became a sacred space where she could confront her grief without fear or judgment. Her canvases told the story of her healing journey, piece by piece. Sometimes, she became so immersed in painting that time seemed to stand still. It wasn't always easy—some days, the pain was too raw—but each time she picked up the brush, she felt a little more connected to herself and her emotions. The process was messy and imperfect, but it was real, and it was hers.

Sharing her artwork became another step in her healing. She started posting some of her pieces online, and to her surprise, people responded. Messages poured in from strangers who had experienced similar losses, sharing their own stories and connecting with her art in a deeply personal way. Evelyn realized she wasn't alone in her grief; she had found a community of people who understood her pain. Her paintings became a bridge—connecting her to others and creating a space for mutual support and understanding. Evelyn's journey taught her that healing isn't about forgetting—it's about finding a way to live alongside the pain. Through art, she discovered a new language for grief, one that allowed her to honor her loved one's memory while also moving forward. The peace she found wasn't in letting go of the past, but in embracing it and allowing it to shape her into someone stronger and more compassionate.

Her story is a powerful testament to the healing power of creativity. If you're struggling with grief or pain, consider exploring a creative outlet—whether it's painting, writing, music, or any form of expression that speaks to you. You don't have to be an artist; you just have to be willing to start. Let your creativity be a space where you can process your emotions and begin to heal. I can personally relate to Evelyn's story. I never truly understood the power of creative healing until I started writing stories. At first, I believed I had lost love when my girlfriend walked away, but through nurturing inner love and cultivating self-awareness, I found a deeper love in writing. When I am fully engaged in writing, time seems to disappear—a feeling of pure flow and connection.

Take action today. Pick up a paintbrush, a pen, an instrument—whatever calls to you—and allow yourself the freedom to create without judgment. Your art doesn't have to be perfect; it just has to be true. Through creative expression, you may find the peace, clarity, and connection you've been searching for. Your journey to healing begins with a single stroke, a single note, a single word. Let your heart guide you—and see where your creativity takes you.

Embracing the Healing Journey

Healing past wounds is a crucial step in the journey of inner love. By acknowledging and accepting your emotions, seeking professional help, practicing self-compassion, engaging in creative expression, and embracing mindfulness, you can begin to heal. Forgiveness, both of others and yourself, plays a vital role in this process, freeing you from the weight of past pain.

Remember, healing is not a linear journey, but a path filled with ups and downs. Be patient and gentle with yourself as you navigate this process. Celebrate the small victories and learn from the setbacks. Your efforts to heal and cultivate inner love will lead to profound personal growth and a more fulfilling life.

CHAPTER 7

BUILDING POSITIVE RELATIONSHIPS

How Inner Love Influences External Relationships

The Ripple Effect

"Love all, trust a few, do wrong to none." – William Shakespeare

Imagine dropping a pebble into a still pond and watching the ripples expand outward. This is how inner love influences our external relationships. When we cultivate inner love and respect for ourselves, it radiates outward, shaping the way we interact with others.

Absolute inner love is like electricity—a boundless source of energy that can power anything. Just as you can plug in any device and expect it to function, inner love fuels every aspect of your life, making whatever you dedicate yourself to flourish. Whether it's relationships, work, or personal growth, when love is the foundation, everything flows effortlessly and transcends into all areas of life.

I remember a time when I struggled with self-esteem. My relationships were filled with misunderstandings and conflicts because I constantly sought validation and approval, as discussed in Chapter One. However, as I began to nurture inner love, I noticed a profound shift. My relationships became healthier, more supportive, and deeply fulfilling. The more love I cultivated within, the more it naturally reflected in my interactions with others. Inner love is not just a feeling—it's a force that transforms everything it touches. By embracing it fully, we create a ripple effect that extends far beyond ourselves, positively impacting the world around us.

The Foundation of Healthy Relationships
Inner love acts as the foundation upon which healthy relationships are built. When you love and respect yourself, you set the standard for how others should treat you. This inner love fosters confidence and self-worth, allowing you to enter relationships from a place of wholeness rather than neediness. It also enables you to recognize and appreciate the worth in others, leading to more authentic and meaningful connections.

The Mirror Effect
Our external relationships often reflect our internal state. If we are critical and unkind to ourselves, we may unconsciously attract relationships that mirror this negativity—ones filled with doubt, insecurity, or emotional imbalance. Conversely, when we cultivate inner love and self-compassion, we naturally draw in positive, supportive relationships that reflect our inner worth.

Even the way we listen to others can serve as a mirror. The conversations we engage in often reveal clues about our inner state—highlighting recurring thoughts, emotions, or internal dialogues we may not have fully acknowledged. When we become aware of these reflections, we gain valuable insights into our own growth and healing journey.

By nurturing inner-love and self-awareness, we reshape the relationships we attract and create a more fulfilling, harmonious external world—one that reflects the love we have cultivated within.

The Impact of Inner Love on Friendships

Laura had always found herself caught in toxic friendships—relationships where she felt disrespected, undervalued, and emotionally drained. No matter how many times she tried to start fresh, she kept attracting people who treated her poorly. Deep down, she knew the root of the problem lay in her own sense of self-worth. Laura struggled with cultivating inner love, often prioritizing others' needs over her own and accepting far less than she deserved.

One evening, seeking a distraction from the heaviness she felt, Laura found herself mindlessly scrolling through social media. A video from a guru she had never seen before caught her attention. The guru spoke about the law of attraction—how the energy we put out into the world is reflected back to us. His message was simple yet profound: "To attract better, you must first believe you deserve better." Those words stopped Laura in her tracks. It felt like a lightbulb moment, as if the universe was nudging her toward a new path. The guru continued, explaining that inner love is the foundation for attracting positive relationships. "By valuing and respecting yourself from within, you naturally raise your standards and align with people who reflect that same energy." For the first time, Laura saw the connection—she had been settling for less because, deep down, she didn't believe she was worthy of more. The message resonated deeply, sparking a shift in her mindset. She realized that the change she desired in her friendships couldn't start with others—it had to begin within her.

Determined to break free from old patterns, Laura committed to a journey of inner love and self-growth. She started small: Practicing daily affirmations to rewire her beliefs about self-worth. Journaling to reflect on her past friendships—not with anger, but with the intention of understanding the patterns that kept her stuck. Setting boundaries to protect her energy and ensure she only allowed mutually supportive connections into her life.

As Laura continued to nurture her inner love, something remarkable happened. The more she valued herself, the more her external world began to shift. She found the courage to distance herself from toxic people and, in doing so, created space for healthier, genuine friendships. Slowly but surely, she began attracting relationships that were kind, uplifting, and respectful**. The change didn't happen overnight, but with every step she took toward inner love, she noticed her circle transforming. The people she met started to mirror the respect and care she was finally showing herself.

Laura's journey is a powerful reminder of how the law of attraction works when rooted in inner love. By elevating her self-worth, she naturally drew in relationships that reflected the energy she cultivated within. She learned that the quality of her friendships wasn't just about who she met—it was about who she became. If you've been struggling with toxic friendships or unfulfilling relationships, take inspiration from Laura's story. Start with inner love. Set small boundaries. Practice kindness toward yourself. Believe that you are worthy of positive, supportive connections. As you shift your inner world, your outer world will begin to reflect those changes. This is how the law of attraction takes shape, aligning your energy with what you truly desire.

When I embodied love and committed to spreading the power of inner love, I began to witness synchronicities—other people started talking about love, even in the most subtle, chance conversations. The more love I radiated, the more love I encountered. Let Laura's story inspire you to take action today. Cultivate inner love, raise your standards, and watch as the relationships in your life align with your deepest desires. You have the power to attract the connections you deserve—and it all begins with the love you give to yourself.

7.1 Identifying and Nurturing Supportive Relationships

Recognizing Supportive Relationships

Take a moment to reflect on the people in your life—the ones whose presence lights up your spirit just by being in the same room, who listen with their hearts, not just their ears, and who remind you of your strength when you've forgotten. These are your tribe—the souls who see you not just for who you are, but for who you're becoming. They hold space for your growth, your dreams, and even your messes, offering the kind of support that nurtures your journey like the most precious of gardens.

But here's the truth: Not everyone is meant to walk with you through every part of your journey. Some will support you from a distance, while others may naturally drift away, making space for new, more aligned connections. And that's okay.

It's also okay to set boundaries with those who drain your energy, cloud your light with negativity, or fail to see you for the incredible person you are. Boundaries aren't about shutting people out—they're about protecting the space where you can thrive. Surround yourself with those who lift you up, who challenge you in healthy ways, and who love you for your authentic self. Your tribe is out there, waiting to grow with you.

Supportive relationships are those that uplift, encourage, and nurture your growth. They are built on mutual respect, trust, and understanding. To identify supportive relationships, look for the following characteristics:

1. **Mutual Respect**: Both parties' value and respect each other's opinions, boundaries, and individuality.
2. **Trust:** There is a foundation of trust, where both parties feel safe and secure.
3. **Encouragement**: Supportive relationships encourage personal growth and celebrate each other's successes.

4.**Empathy:** Both parties show empathy and understanding, especially during difficult times.

Exercise: Relationship Audit

This exercise will help you identify which relationships are truly supportive and which may need re-evaluation.

Take some time to reflect on your current relationships.

Fill in the table below.

Relationship Audit activity

Relationship Name	Respect Boundaries and Opinions (Yes/No)	Feeling safe and Secure (Yes/No)	Encourage and Support (Yes/No)	Personal Growth (Yes/No)	Show Empathy and Understanding (Yes/No)

Nurturing Supportive Relationships

Once you've identified supportive relationships, it's important to nurture them. Here are four tips:

1. **Communicate Openly:** Honest and open communication is key to maintaining healthy relationships. Share your thoughts and feelings and encourage others to do the same.
2. **Show Appreciation:** Regularly express gratitude and appreciation for the people in your life. Small gestures, such as a heartfelt thank-you note or a thoughtful message, can go a long way in strengthening relationships. I remember a friend who truly inspired me—after I expressed my gratitude for the incredible work he does in the community, he shared his future projects with me. His openness reminded me of the power of appreciation; when we acknowledge others, we often receive inspiration and connection in return.
3. **Be Present:** Make an effort to be present and attentive when spending time with loved ones. Put away distractions and focus on truly connecting.
4. **Support Each Other:** Offer your support and encouragement, especially during challenging times. Celebrate each other's successes and be a source of comfort during difficulties.

Nurturing a Lifelong Friendship

Tom and Jake had been inseparable since childhood, sharing countless adventures and supporting each other through thick and thin. They were more like brothers than friends, and their bond seemed unbreakable. But as they grew older, the demands of adulthood—careers, relationships, and daily responsibilities—gradually pulled them in different directions. Their once effortless connection started to fade, reduced to occasional texts and fleeting interactions on social media. Tom missed the easy camaraderie they once had, but he didn't know how to bridge the growing distance.

One day, while scrolling through old photos of the two of them laughing at some long-forgotten joke, Tom felt a pang of nostalgia. He realized just how much he missed Jake's presence in his life. He understood that friendships, like all relationships, need nurturing to survive. In that moment, he made a decision—he wouldn't let their bond slip away. He resolved to take action and make a conscious effort to reconnect.

Tom started with a simple text, checking in on Jake and seeing how he was doing. To his surprise, Jake responded enthusiastically, happy to hear from him. From that point forward, Tom made it a priority to reach out regularly, even if it was just a quick message or a funny meme that reminded him of their shared past. He began planning occasional meet-ups—grabbing coffee, catching a game, or simply hanging out like they used to. Each time they met, it felt as though no time had passed, and Tom was reminded of just how much their friendship meant to him.

Of course, life's busyness didn't suddenly disappear. There were times when plans fell through, or weeks passed without a word. But Tom remained committed, understanding that maintaining a friendship required consistency and effort. He made a point to be there for Jake, not just in the good times, but during the tough moments too—offering a listening ear, sharing advice, or simply being present. Jake, in turn, began to reciprocate. He reached out to Tom more often, planned their next meet-up, and made sure to check in when he knew Tom was going through a rough patch. Their friendship, once at risk of fading into distant memories, began to flourish anew. The effort they both put in didn't just restore what they once had—it deepened their connection, creating a bond that felt even stronger and more supportive than before.

Tom's journey with Jake is a powerful reminder that relationships don't thrive on autopilot—they require care, attention, and intention. If you've noticed a friendship slipping away, take a lesson from Tom's story. Don't wait for the other person to make the first move. Reach out, make plans, and show up. Even small, consistent efforts can rekindle a fading connection and turn it into something meaningful and enduring.

This reminds me of a conversation I had with a friend. He told me, "I lost my mother and went for the burial, and at the same time, my other friend—who lives just a few miles away—also lost his dad. We both attended the burials, but since we returned, we haven't spoken." He hesitated before adding, "I fear reaching out. I don't know what's going on with him."

I looked at him and said, "Do you realize he might be having the same thoughts? Maybe he's waiting for you to reach out first."

He paused, considering my words. "You might be right," he said, a look of realization crossing his face. "I'm going to call him immediately."

Friendships are one of life's greatest gifts, but they require nurturing to truly flourish. Let Tom's experience—and my friend's realization—inspire you to take action today. Reconnect with an old friend, plan that long-overdue catch-up, or simply let someone know you're thinking of them. By investing in the people who matter, you'll not only strengthen your relationships but also enrich your own life in ways you never imagined. It's never too late to nurture the friendships that matter most.

Setting Healthy Boundaries

The Importance of Boundaries

Healthy boundaries are essential for maintaining positive relationships and protecting your well-being. Boundaries help define what is acceptable and unacceptable behavior, ensuring that your needs and limits are respected.

Four Types of Boundaries

1. **Emotional Boundaries:** Protect your emotional well-being by expressing your feelings and setting limits on how others can treat you.
2. **Physical Boundaries:** Define your personal space and comfort levels with physical contact.
3. **Time Boundaries:** Manage your time and commitments by setting limits on how much time you spend on different activities and with different people.
4. **Mental Boundaries:** Protect your thoughts, beliefs, and values by confidently asserting your right to your own opinions and perspectives while respecting those of others.

Fill in Exercise

Boundary-Setting Letter

Dear [*Recipient's Name*],

I hope this message finds you well. I wanted to have an open and honest conversation with you about something that has been on my mind.

Recently, I have noticed that [*describe the specific situation where your boundaries are being crossed, e.g., you frequently request my time for various activities*]. While I deeply value our [*relationship/friendship/work relationship*], I have been feeling [*describe your feelings, e.g., overwhelmed and stressed*] because of this.

It's important for me to maintain a balance in my life and ensure that I have enough personal time to recharge and focus on my well-being. Therefore, I feel it's necessary to set a boundary regarding [*specific situation, e.g., the frequency of our meetups*].

I want to be clear and respectful in communicating this boundary:

> [*state your boundary clearly, e.g., "I value our friendship, but I need some personal time to recharge. I can't meet up every weekend, but I'd love to plan something special once a month."*].

I hope you understand that this boundary is not a reflection of my feelings toward you but rather a step I need to take for my own well-being. I believe that setting this boundary will help me maintain a healthier balance and ultimately strengthen our relationship.

Thank you for understanding and respecting my needs. I look forward to continuing our [*relationship/friendship/work relationship.*] in a way that is supportive and fulfilling for both of us.

With appreciation and respect,

[*Your Name*]

Practice reading out the letter loud, focusing on maintaining a calm and assertive tone and if comfortable share a conversation of this letter to a friend you trust to get their perspective.

Setting health Boundaries with Compassion

Emily and Jackie had been close friends for years, sharing laughter, secrets, and countless late-night conversations. They were each other's confidants, and Emily cherished their bond deeply. But over time, Emily began to notice a shift in their friendship. Jackie, who was going through a rough patch, leaned heavily on Emily for emotional support. What started as occasional heart-to-heart talks turned into daily venting sessions that left Emily feeling overwhelmed and drained.

Emily wanted to be there for Jackie—she cared deeply and genuinely wanted to help. But as the weeks turned into months, Emily realized that constantly shouldering Jackie's burdens was taking a toll on her own mental and emotional well-being. She was losing sleep, feeling anxious, and finding it hard to focus on her own needs. Emily knew something had to change, but the thought of setting boundaries felt daunting. She feared that saying no would hurt Jackie or damage their friendship.

One evening, after yet another exhausting conversation, Emily found herself reflecting on the importance of self-care. She realized that by not setting boundaries, she was not only neglecting her own needs but also enabling an unhealthy dynamic that wasn't truly helping Jackie either. Emily understood that boundaries weren't about pushing people away; they were about creating space for healthier, more balanced relationships. She decided it was time to take action—not just for her own sake, but for the sake of their friendship.

With compassion and honesty, Emily approached Jackie. She gently explained that while she deeply cared for her and valued their friendship, she also needed to set some limits to protect her own well-being. Emily expressed her desire to continue supporting Jackie, but she also encouraged her to seek additional help, like talking to a therapist or exploring other resources. She assured Jackie that this wasn't about rejecting her or the friendship—it was about making sure that they both had the support they needed.

To Emily's relief, Jackie responded with understanding. She appreciated Emily's honesty and realized that relying solely on one friend for all her emotional needs wasn't sustainable or fair. Together, they discussed ways to maintain their friendship without compromising Emily's well-being. Jackie agreed to explore other avenues for support, and Emily felt a weight lift off her shoulders. By setting boundaries with compassion, Emily was able to maintain her friendship with Jackie while also taking care of her own needs.

Emily's journey is a powerful reminder that setting boundaries isn't about shutting people out; it's about honoring your own limits and creating space for healthier, more supportive connections. If you're feeling overwhelmed by the demands of a relationship, take a lesson from Emily's story. Setting boundaries doesn't mean you care any less—it means you care enough to protect both yourself and the integrity of your relationship.

Boundaries are an act of self-respect and a way to ensure that you can continue showing up fully and authentically for the people you love. Let Emily's experience inspires you to take action. Have the conversation, set the limit, and remember that true friends will understand and respect your need for balance. By setting boundaries with compassion, you not only preserve your own well-being but also nurture healthier, more fulfilling relationships. Your needs matter and taking care of yourself is the first step toward taking care of those you care about.

Building a Network of Positive Relationships

Building positive relationships is a crucial aspect of cultivating inner love. When you love and respect yourself, it influences how you interact with others, leading to healthier and more fulfilling connections. Identifying and nurturing supportive relationships, and setting healthy boundaries, are essential steps in this process.

Remember, the quality of your relationships significantly impacts your overall well-being. By surrounding yourself with supportive and positive people, you create an environment that fosters growth, happiness, and inner peace.

Ready to explore strategies for sustaining inner love over time? Let's continue this journey together in the next chapter and discover how to maintain inner love amidst life's inevitable ups and downs. It's time to embrace long-term strategies for a fulfilling and balanced life.

CHAPTER 8

SUSTAINING INNER LOVE

Strategies for Maintaining Inner Love Over Time

The Garden of Inner Love

Imagine that inner love is like a garden. You begin by clearing out the weeds, turning the soil, and preparing the ground with care before planting your seeds. You ensure they have the right soil, sunlight, and water to grow. But as with any garden, this is just the beginning. Gardens require ongoing attention—regular weeding, watering, and protection from pests—to truly flourish. Similarly, inner love demands consistent nurturing and care. I remember a time when I felt confident and content, only to realize that neglecting my self-care had allowed old insecurities to creep back in, leaving me drained and disconnected. It was a stark reminder that inner love is not a one-time achievement but a lifelong commitment.

Cultivating inner love is about creating sacred rituals that nourish every part of you—body, mind, and soul. Neglecting one inevitably takes a toll on the others, which is why a holistic approach to well-being is essential. Think of it as your personal toolkit for maintaining balance, joy, and resilience in a world that constantly demands your attention.

Start by tuning in to what truly feeds your spirit. Maybe it's the quiet moments spent journaling with a hot cup of tea, the exhilarating rush of a morning run as the sun rises, or the deep belly laughs shared with loved ones around a dinner table. Whatever it is, make time for it. Schedule these moments as you would any important meeting—because they are. These moments are not optional; they are your lifeline back to yourself.

As you craft your self-care routine, ask yourself:

1. What brings me peace?

2. What makes me feel alive?

3. What helps me connect to my true self?

Then, build your days around those answers. Your soul deserves to be nourished daily.

Daily Habits for Sustaining Inner Love

"The journey of a thousand miles begins with one step." – Lao Tzu

To maintain Inner love, it's essential to integrate nurturing practices into your daily routine. Here are some habits that can help sustain your Nurturing Inner love journey.

1. Mindfulness and Meditation

Regular mindfulness and meditation practice can help you stay connected to your inner self, fostering ongoing self-awareness and acceptance.

Exercise: Daily Mindfulness Practice

1. Set aside 5-10 minutes each morning for mindfulness meditation.
2. Sit comfortably, close your eyes, and focus on your breath.
3. As you breathe in, mindfully say, "I am enough."
4. As you breathe out, mindfully say, "I am at peace."
5. As you breathe in, mindfully say, "I am capable of _____"
6. As you breathe out, mindfully say, "I release all _____"
7. As you breathe in, mindfully say, "I embrace _____"
8. As you breathe out, mindfully say, "I let go of _____"
9. As you breathe in, mindfully say, "I am grateful for _____
10. As you breathe out, mindfully say, "I forgive _____"
11. As you breathe in, mindfully say, "I welcome _____"

12. As you breathe out, mindfully say, "I surrender to _____"

2. Gratitude Journaling
Maintaining gratitude journaling helps shift your focus from what's lacking in your life to what's abundant, reinforcing a positive mindset.

3. Self-Compassion Practices
Continuing to practice self-compassion helps you navigate life's challenges with kindness and understanding.

Exercise

The Compassionate Pause
1. When you face a setback or make a mistake, take a moment to pause.
2. Place your hand over your heart and take a deep breath.
3. mindfully repeat to yourself: "It's okay. I'm doing my best. I am worthy of love and compassion."
4. Allow yourself to feel the warmth and kindness of these words. Gently bring your awareness to the feeling of love within your heart, letting it expand and fill you with a sense of peace and compassion.

4. Regular Self-Care

Make self-care a non-negotiable priority in your life. Engaging in regular self-care activities—whether it's exercise, mindful eating, or immersing yourself in a beloved hobby—nurtures not only your body but also fuels your mind and spirit, fostering a deeper and more sustained sense of well-being.

For me, each morning begins with either meditation or a jog. As I run or meditate, my mind starts to wander, exploring different thoughts and ideas. It's during these moments of movement and mindfulness that inspiration often strikes. A topic I've been contemplating might suddenly connect with something I heard on a podcast, aligning perfectly with the subject I'm working on. In these moments of flow, clarity emerges effortlessly.

When I return home, the first thing I do is write down these thoughts, capturing them before they fade. I then spend time refining and expanding on them, allowing them to take shape. Many of these insights eventually find their way into my writing, enriched by the unexpected connections that arise when I give my mind the freedom to explore.

From personal experience, I've learned that self-care isn't just about rest—it's about creating space for your mind to breathe, explore, and grow. It is in these quiet, intentional moments that creativity and insight often flourish. By prioritizing regular self-care, you open yourself up to new ideas, deeper creativity, and a more balanced, inspired life.

8.1 The Self-Care Schedule

Ensuring that self-care is a priority in your life is essential for sustained well-being. Engaging in regular self-care activities—such as exercise, healthy eating, and immersing yourself in hobbies—not only nurtures your body but also boosts your mental and emotional health, contributing to greater overall happiness. Research in psychology supports this, showing that regular exercise and mindful self-care practices lead to a healthier, more fulfilling life. To help make self-care a consistent part of your routine, consider creating a personalized self-care schedule that reflects your needs and passions.

Step-by-Step Guide

Step 1. Identify Your Self-Care Activities

List activities that nurture your body, mind, and soul. Think about what makes you feel relaxed, energized, and happy.

Body: Examples include yoga, jogging, dancing, or a relaxing bath.

Mind: Examples include reading, meditation, puzzles, or learning a new skill.

Soul: Examples include hobbies, spending time in nature, journaling, or connecting with loved ones.

Step 2. Create a Weekly Schedule

Use the template below to plan your self-care activities for each day of the week. Be realistic about your time and commitments.

Template

Day	Morning Activity	Afternoon Activity	Evening activity
Monday			
Tuesday			
Wednesday			
Thursday			
Friday			
Saturday			
Sunday			

Step 3. Set Reminders

Set Reminders on your phone or calendar to ensure you stick to your self-care schedule. Treat these activities as non-negotiable appointments with yourself.

Exercise

Step 4: Reflect and Adjust

At the end of each week, reflect on your self-care routine. Ask yourself:

What activities made you feel the best?

_____
_____
_____

Were there any activities that felt like a chore?

_____
_____
_____

How can you adjust your schedule to better meet your needs?

_____
_____
_____

Make adjustments to your schedule for the following week based on your reflections.

_____
_____
_____

Step 5. Share and Support

Share your self-care schedule with a friend or family member. Encourage them to create their own schedule and support each other in maintaining these routines.

Join a self-care group or community where you can share tips, experiences, and encouragement.

Daily Self-Care Check-In

Evening Reflection (5-10 minutes)

Take a few minutes each day to check in with yourself. Use the following prompts to guide your reflection:

1. How am I feeling today?
2. If not in a good mood, what can I do differently tomorrow to feel better?
3. Did I complete my scheduled self-care activities?
4. If not, why?
5. How can I make sure that I stick to my commitment?
6. What can I do tomorrow to improve my well-being?

Weekly Self-Care Reflection

At the end of each week, take some time to journal your thoughts about your self-care routine with the following steps: Reflect on your experiences, celebrate your successes, and plan for any changes you want to make.

1. Set the Scene

    Find a quiet, comfortable place where you can reflect without distractions.

    Gather your favorite journal, pen, and any relaxing items like a cup of tea, calming music, or a cozy blanket.

2. Reflect on Your Experiences

What were the highlights of my self-care routine this week?

_____

_____

What challenges did I face in sticking to my self-care schedule?

_____

_____

3. Celebrate Your Successes

What successes and achievements can I celebrate?

_____

_____

_____

Activity: Reward yourself for your successes. Treat yourself to something special, like a favorite snack, a relaxing bath, or extra time on a hobby you love.

4. Plan for Changes

What changes do I want to make to my self-care routine for next week?

_____
_____
_____

How can I overcome the challenges I faced?

_____
_____
_____

5. Set Goals for the Upcoming Week:

What are my self-care goals for next week?

_____
_____
_____

Activity: Create a visual reminder of your goals. Use sticky notes, a vision board, or digital reminders to keep your goals in mind throughout the week.

6. Interactive Sharing

Who can I share my self-care successes and plans with for accountability and support?

_____
_____
_____

Activity: Reach out to this person or group, share your reflections, and encourage them to join you in the self-care journey.

Stick to this schedule, treating these self-care appointments as non-negotiable.

5. Connecting with Supportive People

Surround yourself with positive, uplifting individuals who encourage your growth, especially those you respect and admire. The right connections can inspire, challenge, and support you in becoming the best version of yourself.

Exercise: The Supportive Circle

1.Make a list of friends and loved ones who support and uplift you.
   1.

2.
   3.
   4.

2. Schedule regular with these individuals—whether through calls, messages, or meet-ups. Consistent connection fosters mutual respect, deepens relationships, and reinforces your commitment to both of them and you.

3. Share your inner love journey with them and encourage mutual support.

Overcoming Setbacks and Staying Committed to the Journey
Facing Setbacks with Resilience
Setbacks are inevitable on any journey, including the path to sustained inner love. It's essential to approach these challenges with resilience and self-compassion.

1. **Recognize and Accept Setbacks**
When setbacks occur, acknowledge them without judgment. Understand that they are a natural part of the journey and do not define your worth.

Exercise: The Setback Reflection
   1. When you experience a setback, take time to reflect on it.

2. Use the prompts below to guide your reflection. Be honest and open with yourself.

Reflection Prompts
1. Describe the Setback
   1. What happened? _____
   2. How did it happen? (Reflect on prior actions or decisions) Be honest_____
   3. When did it happen? _____
   4. Who was involved? _____

2. Emotional Impact
   1. How did this setback make you feel? _____
   2. Why do you think you felt this way? _____

3. Learning Opportunity
   1. What can you learn from this experience? _____
   2. How can this lesson help you in the future? _____

4. Patterns and Triggers
   1. Identify any recurring patterns or triggers related to this setback. _____
   2. What steps can you take to address or avoid these patterns in the future? _____

5. Action Plan

1. What actionable steps can you take to overcome this setback?
   _____

2. How will you monitor your progress? _____

6. Positive Reframe

1. How can you reframe this setback as an opportunity for growth?
   _____

2. What positive outcomes can arise from this experience?
   _____

7. Support System

1. Who can you reach out to for support or guidance? _____

2. How can they help you? _____

8. Self-Compassion

1. Write an affirmation to remind yourself to be kind and patient with yourself during setbacks. _____

1. Gratitude

1. List three things you are grateful for despite this setback. _____

2. How do these aspects bring balance to your perspective?
   _____

10. Moving Forward

1. What are your next steps? _____

2. How can you ensure that you maintain a positive mindset?
   _____

2. Reaffirm Your Commitment to Inner Love

Remind yourself of the importance of Inner love and why you embarked on this journey in the first place. Reaffirm your commitment to your well-being.

Alex's Commitment to Inner Love

Alex had always been the type to put everyone else first—working long hours, constantly saying yes to extra projects, and squeezing in time for friends and family at the expense of his own well-being. He prided himself on being reliable and dedicated, but beneath the surface, Alex was struggling. The relentless pace and lack of boundaries led him to a breaking point; he found himself exhausted, anxious, and disconnected from the things that once brought him joy. The burnout hit hard, leaving him feeling defeated and questioning his own resilience.

One evening, after yet another sleepless night and an overwhelming day, Alex realized he couldn't continue living on autopilot. He knew he needed to make a change, not just for his own well-being, but to reclaim a sense of inner peace that had been missing for far too long. Alex decided it was time to prioritize himself, to embark on a journey of Inner love and self-care that he had neglected for so long.

Alex began by creating a self-care schedule that fit into his hectic life—a weekly plan that included yoga sessions to calm his mind, cooking healthy meals that nourished his body, and setting aside time for activities that made him feel connected to himself and others. He committed to spending quality time with loved ones, something he realized he had been missing amidst the chaos of his daily grind. He also made room for quiet moments of reflection, whether through journaling or simply sitting in stillness, allowing himself to reconnect with his inner voice.

At first, sticking to this new routine felt like just another item on his never-ending to-do list. But as Alex continued to carve out time for his self-care practices, he noticed subtle yet powerful shifts. He felt more energized, his mood lifted, and the sense of overwhelm began to fade. Even on the busiest days, Alex made a promise to himself: he wouldn't let his self-care be the first thing to go. He learned to say no when needed, to set boundaries at work, and to honor his own needs without guilt.

The commitment wasn't always easy. There were moments when work deadlines loomed, when skipping a yoga class or eating a quick meal on the go seemed tempting. But Alex reminded himself of the toll neglecting his well-being had taken in the past. He realized that resilience wasn't about pushing through at all costs; it was about knowing when to pause, to breathe, and to care for himself with the same dedication he showed to his responsibilities.

Through his journey, Alex discovered that self-care wasn't a luxury—it was a necessity. By prioritizing his own needs, he not only improved his mental and physical health but also became a better version of himself for those around him. He was more present, more patient, and more joyful. Alex's self-care wasn't about grand gestures; it was about consistency, about showing up for himself day after day, even when life got tough.

Alex's story is a testament to the transformative power of committing to your own well-being. If you've been feeling overwhelmed or struggling to find time for self-care, let Alex's journey inspire you. Start small—create a simple self-care schedule that includes activities that nurture your mind, body, and soul. Set boundaries that protect your time and energy and remember that taking care of yourself is not selfish—it's essential.

Take action today. Make a commitment to prioritize self-care, no matter how busy life gets. Whether it's a few minutes of meditation, a walk in nature, or a meal that fuels your body, these small acts add up to a greater sense of resilience and inner peace. Your well-being matters, and by investing in yourself, you're taking the first step toward a healthier, more fulfilling life.

Exercise

The Commitment Letter to You

Writing a commitment letter to yourself is a powerful practice of inner love and self-awareness. This letter serves as a tangible reminder of your dedication to nurturing and caring for yourself. By expressing your thoughts and feelings in writing, you affirm the importance of your relationship with yourself and lay a foundation for ongoing self-compassion and growth.

To begin, allow yourself to embrace vulnerability. Writing this letter is a deeply personal and intimate act, and it requires honesty. Open your heart and let your true feelings flow without judgment. This is your space to acknowledge that you are deserving of love and kindness. The words you write are a testament to your inherent worth and a declaration of your commitment to honoring yourself.

As you reflect on this journey of Inner love, take time to recognize how far you have come. Think about the growth you've experienced, the challenges you've faced, and the joy you've found in learning to care for yourself. Let these reflections guide your writing, allowing you to appreciate the progress you have made and the strength you have discovered within.

With this letter, set clear intentions for how you want to continue nurturing your relationship with yourself. Consider what you wish to cultivate in your life moving forward. Whether it's more kindness, patience, or self-acceptance, be specific about the intentions you are setting. This will create a roadmap for your ongoing journey and keep you anchored in your commitment to yourself.

Remember to celebrate the unique qualities that make you who you are. Embrace your strengths and approach your areas of growth with compassion and understanding. Your commitment letter is not about striving for perfection but about recognizing and appreciating the full spectrum of who you are—the light and the shadows.

Finally, reaffirm your commitment to stay dedicated to this journey of Inner love, even when it feels difficult. Understand that Inner love is not a destination but a continuous, evolving path. This letter is a promise to yourself to remain steadfast in nurturing your well-being, no matter the challenges you may encounter.

Take your time with this exercise. Find a quiet and peaceful space where you can reflect and write without distractions. Let your heart guide your words and know that this letter is more than just an exercise—it is a meaningful step toward deepening your relationship with yourself. By committing to this practice, you are embracing a journey toward greater self-awareness, compassion, and inner love.

The Commitment Letter Template

Dear [*Your Name*],
I am writing this letter to reaffirm my commitment to Inner love and to remind myself of the importance of nurturing and caring for the most significant relationship in my life—the one with myself.

Inner love is the cornerstone of my well-being. It is the foundation upon which I build my confidence, resilience, and happiness. When I love myself, I create a life filled with joy, compassion, and inner peace. It allows me to face challenges with strength and embrace my imperfections with grace.

The journey to inner love has profoundly impacted my life in numerous ways. It has taught me to set healthy boundaries, prioritize my needs, and cultivate a sense of worthiness that does not rely on external validation. Inner love has been my anchor during storms, providing me with the stability and comfort I need to navigate through life's ups and downs.

By practicing Inner love, I have become more attuned to my emotions and more forgiving of my mistakes. I have learned to celebrate my achievements, no matter how small, and to view setbacks as opportunities for growth. Inner love has empowered me to pursue my passions, to connect deeply with others, and to live authentically.

I commit to continuing this journey of self-awareness and inner love. I will nurture myself with kindness, patience, and compassion. I will honor my needs and listen to my inner voice and heart. I will celebrate my uniqueness and embrace my journey with an open and loving heart.

With love and commitment,

[Your Name]

NOTE: Re-read this letter whenever you need a reminder of your dedication to the journey of self-awareness.

3. Seek Support When Needed

Don't hesitate to reach out to friends, family, or professionals when facing challenges. An outside perspective can offer valuable insights, encouragement, and clarity, helping you navigate obstacles with greater confidence and direction.

Grace's Supportive Circle

Grace was the kind of person who always put others first. Whether at work, with family, or among friends, she was the go-to person—always ready to lend a helping hand, offer a listening ear, or provide support at a moment's notice. But in her endless giving, she often neglected her own needs. She found herself running on empty, feeling drained, unappreciated, and disconnected from her own sense of worth. As she embarked on her inner love journey, Grace knew she needed to make a change, but she wasn't sure where to start. One day, while searching online for ways to nurture inner love and self-awareness, Grace stumbled upon a local self-care meet-up group. The group promised a supportive community of individuals committed to personal growth and well-being. Though hesitant at first—worried about opening up to strangers and stepping outside her comfort zone—Grace decided to take a leap of faith. She realized that to truly prioritize herself, she needed to surround herself with people who shared her commitment to self-discovery and personal growth.

Walking into her first meet-up, Grace felt a mix of nerves and excitement. She listened as others shared their stories, struggles, and triumphs. It was a room full of individuals, each on their own journey but united by a common goal: to nurture their inner selves. Grace was struck by the openness and vulnerability of those around her. She realized that she wasn't alone in her feelings of overwhelm and self-neglect. Here was a space where it was okay to be imperfect, to have needs, and to prioritize herself without guilt.

As Grace continued to attend the meetups, she began to form deep connections with people who uplifted and inspired her. They exchanged self-care tips, celebrated each other's progress, and provided encouragement during tough times. These friendships became a cornerstone of her inner love practice, showing her that surrounding herself with supportive, like-minded individuals wasn't just beneficial—it was essential.

The relationships Grace nurtured within this circle became a powerful source of strength. They reminded her that inner love wasn't always a solitary journey—it thrived on connection and mutual support. She began to see herself through the eyes of her new friends—worthy, deserving, and capable of giving herself the same love she so freely offered to others. Together, they navigated the ups and downs of their journeys, proving that the power of community could be truly transformative.

I personally recall my first encounter with my friend Jackson. When I first met him, he was tall and slender, a quiet presence in my life. Then, for about five years, he disappeared from my vicinity. When I saw him again, he was completely transformed—his once lean frame now sculpted with impressive muscle. I was taken aback, genuinely pleased with his growth and discipline. As we talked, Jackson introduced me to the world of fitness. He became my workout partner, guiding me through the principles of resilience, focus, and consistency—qualities that have transcended beyond the gym and into my work and personal life.

Grace's experience taught her that to truly embrace inner love, it was crucial to cultivate a supportive environment. The encouragement she received from her new circle helped her stay committed to her self-care routines, even on the days she felt like giving up. She learned that it was okay to ask for help, to lean on others, and to celebrate her progress, no matter how small. These connections brought her joy, resilience, and a renewed sense of purpose.

If it hadn't been for my chance meeting with Jackson, I don't think I would have become who I am today. I learned invaluable lessons in the gym—not just about fitness, but about discipline, perseverance, and self-improvement. His commitment and resilience were deeply inspirational, and his attitude was a powerful source of motivation for my own progress.

Grace's story serves as a reminder that the journey to inner love doesn't have to be traveled alone—though at times, it may feel that way. If you've been struggling to prioritize yourself, consider seeking out a supportive community. Whether it's an inner love meet-up, a self-care group, or simply reconnecting with friends who uplift you, surrounding yourself with positive influences can be a powerful catalyst for change.

Take a step today—find a group, reach out to a friend, or create your own circle of support. Let Grace's journey inspire you to surround yourself with people who see your worth and encourage your growth. Inner love flourishes in connection, and the right support can make all the difference in nurturing your self-awareness and well-being. Embrace the strength that comes from community and take action to build your own supportive circle.

Exercise: The Support Network

I will be calling _____, _____, _____, and _____ to support me during challenging times. How can each of them help you?

_____
_____
_____
_____

2. Reach out to them for advice, encouragement, or simply a listening ear.

Jenna's Journey of Resilience

Jenna had been on her inner love journey for several years, gradually learning to appreciate herself and quiet the harsh inner critic that had long dominated her thoughts. She had made significant progress in nurturing her confidence and embracing herself—flaws and all. But when life threw a series of unexpected challenges her way—losing her job, the end of a meaningful relationship, and mounting stress—Jenna felt like the ground beneath her had crumbled. Suddenly, self-doubt crept back in, and the resilience she had worked so hard to build seemed to vanish overnight. She felt defeated, as though she had been pushed back to square one.

Instead of giving in to despair, Jenna made a courageous decision: to lean even deeper into her inner love practices, especially when it felt hardest. She picked up her inner love journal—a tool that had once been a source of comfort but had been gathering dust on her nightstand. With a shaky hand, she began to write, pouring her fears, frustrations, and vulnerabilities onto the page. Each entry became a safe space where she could process her emotions without judgment, a way to navigate the pain and confusion threatening to consume her.

"It is not the critic who counts; not the man who points out how the strong man stumbles, or where the doer of deeds could have done them better. The credit belongs to the man who is actually in the arena, whose face is marred by dust and sweat and blood." – Theodore Roosevelt

Through journaling, Jenna began to shift her perspective. Her setbacks were not failures; they were part of her journey. She wrote about her dreams, her fears, and the small victories she still found in her days. She reminded herself of the strengths that had carried her through past challenges and reaffirmed her commitment to self-compassion. She filled the pages with affirmations, offering herself kindness even on the days she didn't feel strong or confident. Each entry became a promise: to keep going, to keep loving, and to trust in her ability to rise again.

Jenna also leaned on her support system, reaching out to friends who reminded her of her worth when she struggled to see it herself. They listened, encouraged, and stood by her side, showing her that she didn't have to go through this alone. With every conversation and every word she wrote, Jenna slowly felt her resilience reignite. She realized that setbacks weren't signs of failure but opportunities to deepen her self-awareness and strengthen her inner love.

As she continued journaling and reflecting, the challenges she once viewed as insurmountable began guiding her toward profound growth. She started seeing each struggle as a lesson, a chance to build her resilience and affirm her self-worth. Gradually, her confidence returned, and with it, a renewed sense of purpose. Jenna's journey taught her that inner love wasn't about never falling—it was about finding the strength to rise, again and again. She understood that resilience wasn't a destination but a practice—one that required patience, persistence, and above all, self-compassion.

Jenna's story is a powerful reminder that the path to inner love isn't linear. If you're feeling defeated or struggling to stay resilient, take a lesson from her experience. Pick up a journal and start writing, even if it's just a few words each day. Allow yourself to feel, to reflect, and to nurture the parts of you that need the most compassion. Remember, setbacks are not the end; they are opportunities for deeper growth.

Let Jenna's journey inspire you to take action today. Start your own inner love journal, reach out for support, and reaffirm your commitment to loving yourself through every high and low. Resilience is not about being unbreakable—it's about embracing vulnerability, learning from challenges, and continuing forward with grace and self-love. Every step you take is a step toward becoming the person you are meant to be.

8.3 A Lifelong Commitment

Sustaining inner love is a lifelong commitment. It requires continuous effort, self-awareness, and compassion. The journey is filled with highs and lows, but each step forward brings you closer to a deeper understanding and appreciation of yourself.

As you continue this path, remember that inner love is not a destination but a journey. Embrace the process, celebrate your progress, and be kind to yourself during setbacks. With each day, you are cultivating a garden of inner love that will bloom and thrive, enriching your life and the lives of those around you.

Ready to reflect on the ongoing journey of self-discovery? Let's conclude this transformative journey together by celebrating your achievements and looking forward to a future filled with love, growth, and fulfillment.

Recap of Key Insights and Takeaways

Reflecting on the Journey
As we come to the conclusion of this book, let's take a moment to reflect on the journey we've traveled together. From understanding

the foundational importance of inner love and distinguishing it from narcissism to exploring practical steps for nurturing inner love, we have delved deep into the essence of self-awareness and personal growth.

Key Insights and Takeaways

1. The Power of Inner Love: Inner love is the cornerstone of a fulfilling and balanced life. It provides the strength to overcome challenges and the clarity to make choices that honor your true self.

2. Overcoming Barriers: We all encounter obstacles on the path to inner love—negative self-talk, past traumas, self-image struggles, and societal pressures. Recognizing and addressing these barriers is the first step toward healing, growth, and deeper understanding of oneself.

3. Embracing Vulnerability: Vulnerability is not a sign of weakness but a profound strength. It allows you to connect deeply with yourself and others, fostering genuine relationships and personal authenticity.

4. Daily Practices for Inner Love: Incorporating daily practices like affirmations, meditation, journaling, and self-care routines can help sustain inner love over time. Consistency in these practices is key to maintaining your well-being.

5. Mindfulness and Inner Peace: Mindfulness and meditation enhance self-awareness and inner peace, helping you stay connected to the present moment and embrace your true self with compassion.

6. Healing Past Wounds: Techniques like acknowledging emotions, seeking professional help, practicing self-compassion, and embracing forgiveness are crucial for healing emotional and psychological wounds.

7. Building Positive Relationships: Inner love influences how you interact with others, leading to healthier and more fulfilling relationships. Identifying and nurturing supportive connections, along with setting healthy boundaries, are essential steps in this process.

8. Sustaining Inner love: Maintaining inner love requires ongoing effort and commitment. Overcoming setbacks with resilience and seeking support when needed are vital for staying on track.

Encouragement to Continue your journey

The Lifelong Path of Self-Discovery

As we've explored throughout this book, inner love and self-awareness are lifelong journeys, not fixed destinations. Along the way, you have gained valuable tools and insights to help you navigate this path. These tools are not rigid—they can be adapted to fit your schedule, needs, and personal growth process.

Remember, progress doesn't require giant leaps; small, consistent steps matter just as much. Setbacks are a natural part of growth, but what truly matters is your continued commitment to nurturing your inner love and evolving along the way.

The Ongoing Journey: The pursuit of inner love and self-discovery is akin to a lifelong adventure, filled with both challenges and triumphs. Recognizing that this journey has no fixed endpoint is essential. Instead, it's an evolving process of learning, growth, and transformation. Each day brings new opportunities to deepen your self-awareness and nurture the love within.

Embracing Small Steps: Embracing small steps is essential on this journey. Personal growth doesn't require grand gestures or drastic changes; rather, it thrives on consistency. Small, intentional actions—whether practicing mindfulness, writing in a gratitude journal, or simply allowing yourself to rest—gradually build resilience and create a profound impact over time. Trust that every small effort contributes to lasting transformation.

Handling Setbacks with Grace: Setbacks are inevitable on this journey. When encountering obstacles or doubt, approach them with grace and compassion. View setbacks as opportunities for growth and learning, not failures. Each challenge builds resilience and deepens your understanding of your strengths and limitations.

Commitment to Growth: Your commitment to growth and inner love sustains you. Remember, self-discovery isn't linear; there will be ups and downs. Your dedication to nurturing inner love guides you through difficult times. Celebrate progress, no matter how small, and remain committed to personal development.

Practical Tools for Sustained Inner Love: This book introduced various tools and practices to support your journey, including mindfulness exercises, reflective journaling, self-compassion techniques, and cultivating supportive relationships. Integrating these practices into your daily routine creates a solid foundation for ongoing self-discovery and inner peace.

The Power of Reflection

Reflection is a powerful tool in the journey of self-discovery. Regularly reflecting on your experiences, thoughts, and emotions helps you gain deeper insights into your true self. This allows you to celebrate achievements, understand challenges, and set intentions for continued growth. Make reflection a regular part of your routine to stay connected with your inner journey.

Building a Supportive Network

Surrounding yourself with supportive, like-minded individuals enhances your self-discovery journey. Positive relationships provide encouragement, accountability, and a sense of community. Seek connections with people who uplift and inspire you and be willing to offer the same support in return. This creates a network that fosters mutual growth and understanding.

Embracing the Journey

I walked into the gym with a simple goal: to regain my strength and, maybe, become more attractive to women. What I didn't realize was that I had stepped into a crucible of Nurturing inner love—physically, mentally, and spiritually. The gym became more than a place to lift weights and break a sweat; it was a sanctuary where my body and spirit became one, reshaping my identity with each step. It wasn't just a physical space; it was a mirror, reflecting me back to myself—unmasked, unfiltered—pushing me to confront my limitations and unearth my potential.

I began to see the gym as a sculptor's studio, where I was both the artist and the clay. Every workout became a deliberate act of creation, chiseling away at insecurities and doubt, revealing a version of myself I had only imagined. But it wasn't just about sculpting my body—it was about shaping my character. With each challenge I overcame, I grasped the true meaning of perseverance, discipline, and resilience. The patience I practiced waiting for results, the grit I summoned to push through the last rep, and the resilience I found in the face of setbacks became a training ground for life's greater battles.

The gym taught me a profound truth: when you commit to pushing yourself, to overcoming resistance, life itself begins to flow with greater ease. This is why people often say time disappears when they're deeply engaged in something they love—whether it's making art, pursuing a dream, or even making love. In those moments, the illusion of separation dissolves, and something deeper takes over—a state of absolute presence. Perhaps that's the only time the idea of a soulmate truly makes sense—when two people merge in intimacy, unbound by time or space, becoming one in the purest sense.

Once you transcend space and time in your own consciousness, what remains is love. Your consciousness is a microcosm of the vast, universal consciousness—just as the gym is a microcosm of life's struggles. The beauty lies in mastering the art of navigating these struggles, transcending them into a higher state of being. I found this same realization echoed in the words of Jeff Bezos. In a podcast, he described Earth as a gym—challenging, demanding, shaping us—but once you break through the gravitational pull into the vastness of space, it's pure bliss. The effort, the speed, the sheer energy required to escape gravity and launch into that limitless expanse—it's the same force I felt in nurturing inner love. Just as astronauts experience an overwhelming sense of unity and awareness when they escape Earth's atmosphere, I found that same liberation through disciplined effort, pain, and perseverance.

But the lessons I learned extended beyond the weights and machines. The discipline, dedication, and determination I cultivated in the gym spilled over into every aspect of my life. The gym equipped me with armor to face challenges outside its walls, reminding me that the limits I once saw were mere illusions within my own consciousness. This journey was never just about reaching a destination; it was about embracing the continuous process of becoming. Nurturing inner love is not a single event but a series of daily choices that shape us into who we are meant to be.

If you're standing at the edge, hesitating to begin your own journey, know this—the path to nurturing inner love doesn't demand perfection; it only asks for a start. Step into that space, lift that weight, run that mile, and let the journey sculpt you from the inside out. The gym—or any form of dedicated effort—isn't just about feeling good; it's a testament to your potential, a canvas for your resilience, and a powerful reminder that you are capable of far more than you ever imagined.

Embrace the process, trust the journey, and watch as you transform—not just your body, but your entire being. This is about more than fitness; it's about reclaiming your strength, your power, and your story. The journey begins with a single step—and that step can change everything.

Encouragement to Keep Going

I commend you for taking the courageous step of embarking on the path of self-discovery and inner love. Starting this journey requires bravery, self-awareness, and a willingness to embrace both the light and shadows within. As you continue, remember to practice the techniques and strategies learned throughout this book. These tools - mindfulness, journaling, self-compassion exercises, and supportive relationships - are your allies, guiding and supporting your growth. Use them daily, making them part of your routine, and watch as they transform your life.

On tough days when progress seems slow, seek support from friends, family, or uplifting communities. Don't hesitate to ask for help; external perspectives can provide clarity and encouragement. Remember, seeking support is a strength, not a weakness. Celebrate your progress, no matter how small. Each step, moment of self-reflection, and act of inner love is a victory, building resilience and inner strength. Reflect on your journey and take pride in your progress. You are doing the work, and that's worth celebrating.

Inner love is not a luxury but a necessity, the foundation for resilience, joy, and love. By nurturing inner love, you create a fulfilling life where you can thrive and shine. You are on a transformative journey, filled with ups and downs, but each experience contributes to growth and self-awareness. Embrace this process with an open heart and compassionate spirit.

Trust you are exactly where you need to be and move forward with courage and determination. Your dedication is a testament to your strength and resilience. You deserve love, happiness, and peace. Continue nurturing inner love, and let it guide you toward greater fulfillment and joy. Remember, you are becoming the best version of yourself, and that's truly magnificent.

8.4 The Beauty of Inner Love

In a world that constantly demands our attention and defines our worth by external standards, inner love can feel elusive. Yet, it is the cornerstone of a fulfilling life—a transformative force that allows us to recognize our intrinsic value, embrace our imperfections, and live authentically. Through these seven core principles, inner love empowers us to build meaningful relationships, navigate life's challenges with resilience, and create a foundation for lasting joy, peace, and fulfillment.

1. Recognizing Our Inherent Worth

Inner love begins with acknowledging our inherent worth—not because of what we achieve or possess, but simply because we exist. This realization is profoundly liberating, freeing us from the relentless pursuit of external validation and allowing us to find contentment within ourselves. When we detach our self-worth from societal expectations, we open the door to true self-acceptance and inner peace.

2. Embracing Imperfection

One of the most vital aspects of inner love is embracing our imperfections. Society often pressures us to strive for unattainable perfection, leading to self-doubt and dissatisfaction. True inner love is about recognizing that we are beautifully flawed, unique, and wholly human. By shifting our focus from unrealistic standards to appreciating our strengths, we silence self-criticism and celebrate the qualities that make us special.

3. Living Authentically

Authenticity is another gift of inner love—it grants us the courage to be our true selves, free from the fear of judgment. When we align our actions with our values and beliefs, rather than conforming to external expectations, we cultivate a life of integrity and deep satisfaction. Authentic living fosters stronger, more meaningful relationships built on honesty and mutual respect, enriching our connections with others.

4. Resilience in the Face of Challenges
Inner love also fortifies us with resilience, enabling us to navigate life's inevitable ups and downs with grace. A strong foundation of self-love helps us bounce back from adversity, learn from setbacks, and keep moving forward with strength and determination. When we trust in our ability to grow through life's challenges, we replace fear with confidence and setbacks with opportunities for growth.

5. Cultivating Inner Love
Inner love is not a destination but a continuous journey—one that requires conscious effort and practice. Mindfulness, self-compassion, gratitude, and positive affirmations are powerful tools in this process. By nurturing ourselves daily, we reinforce our self-worth and deepen our connection with our inner being, gradually transforming our outlook on life. Over time, this consistent practice leads to greater joy, peace, and fulfillment.

6. The Triumph of Inner Love

The rewards of inner love extend far beyond personal well-being. When we love ourselves, we radiate positivity, attract enriching experiences, and become magnets for joy and fulfillment. Our relationships flourish, our mental and emotional well-being improves, and we achieve a profound sense of inner harmony. More importantly, inner love empowers us to contribute positively to the world—spreading kindness, understanding, and compassion to those around us.

7. A Life of True Harmony

Inner love is a powerful force that transforms us from the inside out. It allows us to see our worth, embrace our imperfections, and live in alignment with our true selves. More than just a personal journey, it is the foundation for a life of joy, peace, and meaningful relationships. Embracing inner love is not an act of selfishness but a profound acknowledgment of our inherent value—one that enables us to live in true harmony with ourselves and the world.

A Motivational Message

As you continue this journey called life, remember that you are worthy of love and compassion - even when you've eaten an entire pizza by yourself. In a world that often measures worth by Instagram likes and YouTube views recognize that your true value lies within. Your journey is unique, and every step is a testament to your strength and courage.

Embrace both highs and lows, knowing each experience contributes to your growth. Celebrate moments of triumph and happiness but also acknowledge moments of doubt and failure as opportunities for growth. These challenging times reveal your true strength and resilience.

Your journey is uniquely yours, reflecting your individuality. Avoid comparing yourself to others; instead, celebrate your uniqueness. Remember, you are worthy of love and compassion - not just from others, but also from yourself. Inner love and self-compassion are the foundations of a fulfilling life.

Strength and courage can be quiet and subtle, manifesting in everyday choices to persevere and show kindness. Hold onto hope, the light that guides you through difficult times. Hope gives you the strength to keep moving forward, even when the path is uncertain.

Your journey is a testament to your strength and courage. Embrace highs with gratitude and lows with grace, knowing each experience contributes to your growth. Celebrate your individuality, be kind to yourself, and hold onto hope. Your journey is unique and unfolding beautifully. Continue walking your path with confidence, knowing you are strong, capable, and deserving of life's good things.

A Final Affirmation

Repeat this affirmation to yourself: "I am worthy of love. I embrace my journey with compassion and courage. I am enough, just as I am."

Looking Forward

Your journey doesn't end here. It continues with each new day, each new experience, and each act of Inner love. Carry the insights and tools you've gained with you and let them guide you toward a life of greater self-awareness, inner peace, and love. For more information find us at www.nurturinginnerlove.com

Thank You

Thank you for allowing me to be part of your journey. I hope this book has offered you inspiration and guidance to cultivate and sustain inner love—a love that radiates harmoniously into every aspect of your life. Remember, you are never alone on this path. Together, we can create a world where inner love and compassion flourish, leading to a brighter, more connected future.

Best Wishes

May your journey be filled with love, growth, and infinite possibilities. Keep moving forward with an open heart and a courageous spirit. The world needs your light—always let it shine from within, guided by your inner love rather than your mind.

With love and gratitude,
Val Kizza Ssegirinya

REFERENCES

1. Bowers, K., & McDonald, K. (2020). *Creative healing: Art therapy for grief and loss.* Art Therapy Journal, 37(1), 25-32
2. Brown, B. (2010). *The gifts of imperfection: Let go of who you think you're supposed to be and embrace who you are.* Hazelden Publishing.
3. Brown, B. (2012). *Daring greatly: How the courage to be vulnerable transforms the way we live, love, parent, and lead.* Gotham Books.
4. Brown, K. W., & Ryan, R. M. (2003). The benefits of being present: Mindfulness and its role in psychological well-being. *Journal of Personality and Social Psychology, 84*(4), 822-848.
5. Brantley, J. (2011). *The mindfulness solution: Everyday practices for everyday problems.* New Harbinger Publications.
6. Chopra, D. (2018). *The healing self: A revolutionary new plan to supercharge your immunity and stay well for life.* Harmony Books.efgh
7. Cloud, H., & Townsend, J. (2017). *Boundaries: When to say yes, how to say no to take control of your life.* Zondervan.
8. Crocker, J., & Wolfe, C. (2001). Contingencies of self-worth. *Psychological Review, 108*(3), 593-623. https://doi.org/10.1037/0033-295X.108.3.593

9. Deci, E. L., & Ryan, R. M. (2000). The "what" and "why" of goal pursuits: Human needs and the self-determination of behavior. *Psychological Inquiry*, 11(4), 227-268.
10. Dispenza, J. (2017). Becoming Supernatural: How Common People Are Doing the Uncommon. Hay House, Inc.
11. Dwyer, M. (2021). The healing power of relationships: *Understanding the impact of supportive connections.* Journal of Social and Personal Relationships, 38(2), 258-276.
12. Eckhart, M. (2009). *The essential Meister Eckhart* (E. K. Davis, Ed.). Penguin Classics. (Original work published in the 14th century)
13. Emerson, R. W. (1996). *The essays of Ralph Waldo Emerson* (J. M. McFarland, Ed.). St. Martin's Press. (Original work published in 1841)
14. Emunah, R. (2018). Acting on behalf of the heart: *Creative arts therapies for healing trauma and loss.* In C. M. Malchiodi (Ed.), Handbook of art therapy (pp. 153-168). The Guilford Press.
15. Fredrickson, B. L., Cohn, M. A., Coffey, K. A., Pek, J., & Finkel, S. M. (2008). Open hearts build lives: Positive emotions, induced through loving-kindness meditation, build consequential personal resources. *Journal of Personality and Social Psychology,* 95(5), 1045-1062.

https://psycnet.apa.org/doiLanding?doi=10.1037%2Fa00132 62

16. Germer, C. K. (2009). *The mindful path to self-compassion: Freeing yourself from destructive thoughts and emotions.* Guilford Press.

17. Germer, C. K., & Neff, K. D. (2013). Self-compassion in clinical practice. *Journal of Clinical Psychology, 69*(8), 856-867. https://onlinelibrary.wiley.com/doi/10.1002/jclp.22037

18. Ginsburg, K. R., & Jablow, M. M. (2015). *Building resilience in children and teens: Giving kids roots and wings.* American Psychological Association.

19. Gilbert, P. (2009). *The compassionate mind: A new approach to life's challenges.* Constable.

20. Gilbert, P. (2010). *The compassionate mind: A new approach to life's challenges.* Constable.

21. Goleman, D. (1995). *Emotional intelligence: Why it can matter more than IQ.* Bantam Books.

22. Golovey, L., Manukyan, V., Troshihina, E., Aleksandrova, O., &Rykman, L. (2020). *Emotional and Psychological Well-Being of a Person in Difficult Life Situations* (https://typeset.io/papers/emotional-and-psychological-well-being-of-a-person-in-ipj2e5h6ee). Journal Article.

23. Harrison, K. (2021). Navigating social media pressure: The impact on self-esteem. *Journal of Social and Personal*

Relationships, 38(7), 1980-1998. https://doi.org/10.1177/02654075211026977

24. Hayes, S. C., & Strosahl, K. (2004). *A practical guide to acceptance and commitment therapy.* Springer Science & Business Media.

25. Kabat-Zinn, J. (1990). *Full catastrophe living: Using the wisdom of your body and mind to face stress, pain, and illness.* Delacorte Press.

26. Kabat-Zinn, J. (2003). *Mindfulness for beginners: Reclaiming the present moment—and your life.* Sounds True.

27. Kabat-Zinn, J. (2005). *Wherever you go, there you are: Mindfulness meditation in everyday life.* Hachette Books.

28. Kearney, R. (2018). The art of grieving: *How creativity can help us heal.* Journal of Creative Arts in Education, 5(2), 145-158.

29. Kessler, R. C. (2012). *The focus: The secret, the power of vulnerability.* Center for Creative Leadership.

30. Keng, S. L., Smoski, M. J., & Robins, C. J. (2011). Effects of mindfulness on psychological health: A review of empirical studies. *Clinical Psychology Review, 31*(6), 1041-1056. https://www.sciencedirect.com/science/article/abs/pii/S02727 3581100081X?via%3Dihub

31. Miller, W. R., & Rollnick, S. (2013). *Motivational interviewing: Helping people change.* Guilford Press.

32. Mindful. (n.d.). How to practice self-compassion. Retrieved September 25, 2024, from https://www.mindful.org/how-to-practice-self-compassion/
33. Morf, C. C., & Rhodewalt, F. (2001). "Unraveling the Self: Narcissism and Self-Esteem." *In The Self (pp. 60-86). Psychology Press.*
34. Neff, K. D. (2003). Self-compassion: An alternative conceptualization of a healthy attitude toward oneself. *Self and Identity, 2*(2), 85-101. https://www.tandfonline.com/doi/abs/10.1080/15298860309027
35. Neff, K. D. (2011). *Self-compassion: The proven power of being kind to yourself.* William Morrow.
36. Neff, K. D., & Germer, C. K. (2013). A pilot study and randomized controlled trial of the Mindful Self-Compassion program. *Journal of Clinical Psychology, 69*(1), 28-44. https://onlinelibrary.wiley.com/doi/10.1002/jclp.21923
37. Neimeyer, R. A. (2012). *Meaning reconstruction in bereavement: Transforming the experience of loss.* In M. S. Stroebe, R. O. Hansson, H. Schut, & W. Stroebe (Eds.), Handbook of bereavement research and practice: Advances in theory and intervention (pp. 97-123). American Psychological Association

38. Parker, J. (2020). The role of reflective journaling in therapeutic practices. *Journal of Mental Health Counseling, 42*(2), 159-172. https://doi.org/10.17744/mehc.42.2.02
39. Pennebaker, J. W. (1997). *Opening up: The healing power of expressing emotions.* Guilford Press.
40. Rosenberg, M. B. (2003). Nonviolent communication: *A language of life. Puddle.* Dancer Press.
41. Rumi. (n.d.). *The essential Rumi* (translated by Coleman Barks). HarperCollins.
42. Serdiuk, L. (2022). Internal Resources of Personal Psychological Well-Being (https://typeset.io/papers/internal-resources-of-personal-psychological-well-being-1csub53b) . The Global Psychotherapist.
43. Scherer, L. D., & Lichtenstein, S. (2017). The effect of mindfulness meditation on self-compassion: A meta-analysis. *Mindfulness, 8*(6), 1454-1468.
44. Schlosser, A. (2014). Interface entre saúde mental e relacionamento
amoroso: um olhar a partir da psicologia positive (https://typeset.io/papers/interface-entre-saude-mental-e-relacionamento-amoroso-um-3b4xnsad9t).Universidade Federal de Santa Catarina.
45. Shapiro, S. L., Brown, K. W., & Biegel, G. M. (2007). Teaching self-care to caregivers: Effectiveness of a

mindfulness-based intervention. *Journal of Clinical Psychology, 63*(3), 267-277. https://onlinelibrary.wiley.com/doi/10.1002/jclp.20365

46. Siegel, D. J. (2010). *The mindful therapist: A clinician's guide to mindsight and neural integration.* W.W. Norton & Company.

47. Seligman, M. E. P. (2011). *Flourish: A visionary new understanding of happiness and well-being.* Free Press.

48. Shakespeare, W. (2000). *The complete works of William Shakespeare.* (W. J. Rolfe, Ed.). New York: P.F. Collier & Son. (Original work published in 1623)

49. Smith, B. W., & Zautra, A. J. (2008). Resilience: The role of social support and coping strategies. In J. W. Reich, A. J. Zautra, & J. S. Hall (Eds.), *Handbook of adult resilience* (pp. 117-138). Guilford Press.

50. Smith, S. W., & Smith, L. (2017). Building resilience through positive relationships: *Strategies for personal and professional growth.* Journal of Positive Psychology, 12(5), 468-475.

51. Sweeney, P. D. (2020). The importance of self-care: Why caring for yourself is critical to your mental health. *Journal of Mental Health, 29*(1), 1-2.

52. Thich Nhat Hanh. (1991). Peace Is Every Step: *The Path of Mindfulness in Everyday Life.* Bantam Books.

53. Tolle, E. (1999). *The power of now: A guide to spiritual enlightenment*. New World Library.
54. Tolle, E. (2005). *A new earth: Awakening to your life's purpose*. Penguin Group.
55. Twenge, J. M., & Campbell, W. K. (2009). "Narcissism: A Social Disease." *Psychology Today*.
56. Van Dierendonck, D. (2011). Servant leadership: A review and synthesis. *Journal of Management, 37*(4), 1228-1261. https://doi.org/10.1177/0149206310380465
57. Van der Kolk, B. A. (2014). *The body keeps the score: Brain, mind, and body in the healing of trauma*. Penguin Books.
58. Walsh, R., & Shapiro, S. L. (2006). The meeting of meditative disciplines and western psychology: A mutually enriching dialogue. *American Psychologist, 61*(3), 227-239. https://doi.org/10.1037/0003-066X.61.3.227
59. Williams, M. (2019). *Mindfulness: A practical guide to finding peace in a frantic world*. Piatkus.
60. Wilk, M. (2018). *The healing power of creativity: How the arts can help us cope with trauma and emotional pain*. Springer.
61. Neff, K. D., &Germer, C. K. (2013). A pilot study and randomized controlled trial of the Mindful Self-Compassion program. Journal of Clinical Psychology, 69 (1), 28-44.

62. Fredrickson, B. L., Cohn, M. A., Coffey, K. A., Pek, J., & Finkel, S. M. (2008). Open hearts build lives: Positive emotions, induced through loving-kindness meditation, build consequential personal resources. Journal of Personality and Social Psychology, 95 (5), 1045-1062.
63. Serdiuk, L. (2022). Internal Resources of Personal Psychological Well-Being (https://typeset.io/papers/internal-resources-of-personal-psychological-well-being-1csub53b) . The Global Psychotherapist.
64. Siegel, D. J. (2010). *The mindful therapist: A clinician's guide to mindsight and neural integration.* W.W. Norton & Company.
65. Sweeney, P. D. (2020). *The importance of self-care: Why caring for yourself is critical to your mental health.* Journal of Mental Health, 29(1), 1-2
66. Golovey, L., Manukyan, V., Troshihina, E., Aleksandrova, O., &Rykman, L. (2020). Emotional and Psychological Well-Being of a Person in Difficult Life Situations (https://typeset.io/papers/emotional-and-psychological-well-being-of-a-person-in-ipj2e5h6ee) . Journal Article.
67. For further information and more in-depth research, you can visit SciSpace https://typeset.io/search
68. Buddha. (n.d.). Quote commonly attributed to Buddha

Nurturing Inner love

www.nurturinginnerlove.com

Scan Here

To Continue the journey with us

Inner Love & Self-Awareness in depth

Guided Mindfulness & Meditation.

Journaling Prompts

Daily Affirmations

Healing & Growth

Relationships

Nurturing Positive Relationships

Navigating Toxic Relationships

Creative Expression

insights and inspirations

Workshops & Events

Webinars & Online Courses

Reflective Journals & Merchandise

Made in the USA
Columbia, SC
23 April 2025